The
Shopping
Malls *of*
Heaven

The Shopping Malls of Heaven

and the Meaning of Life

by Saeed Kauser

SUBLIME BOOKS

MISSISSAUGA, ONTARIO, CANADA

Copyright © 2016 Saeed Kauser
Second Edition

Published by Sublime Books
Mississauga, Ontario, Canada
www.theshoppingmallsofheaven.com

All rights reserved. The use of any part of this publication reproduced, transmitted in any form or by any means, electronic, mechanical, recording, or otherwise, or stored in a retrieval system, without prior consent of the publisher, is an infringement of the copyright law. In the case of photocopying or other reprographic copying of the material, a license must be obtained from the Canadian Copyright Licensing Agency (CANCOPY) before proceeding.

Library and Archives Canada Cataloguing in Publication

Kauser, Saeed, 1962-, author
    The shopping malls of heaven : and the meaning of life / Saeed Kauser.

Includes bibliographical references.
Issued in print and electronic formats.
ISBN 978-0-9783984-1-5 (hardcover).--
ISBN 978-0-9783984-2-2 (paperback).--
ISBN 978-0-9783984-4-6 (kindle).--
ISBN 978-0-9783984-3-9 (epub)

    1. Paradise--Islam. I. Title.

BP166.87.K39 2016	297.2'3	C2016-900553-4
		C2016-900554-2

Edited by Simone Gabbay
Interior layout and cover design: Simone Gabbay Associates
www.simonegabbay.com

Contents

Preface xi

Introduction xiii
    Significance of the Number Seven xx

Chapter 1
What Is Heaven All About? 1
    Why Did God Create Us? 7
    Why Did God Remove Us from Heaven? 12
    Is Heaven Physical or Spiritual? 21
    Human Psyche 23

Chapter 2
The Period between Life and Afterlife 25
    Sleep............................. 31
    The Barrier 32
    Astral Projection and NDEs 41
    Mairaj—The Prophet's Astral Journey ... 47

Chapter 3
Doomsday and Resurrection 49
   The End of the World 49

   Creation of a New Universe 53

   Resurrection 54

   Judgment 59

   As-Sirat—Bridge over Hell 61

   Hell 63

   Transfer from Hell into Heaven 66

Chapter 4
Properties of Heaven 69
   Size of Heaven 69

   Location of Heaven 72

   Does Heaven Exist Now
   or Will It Be Created Later? 74

   Levels of Heaven 79

   Throne of God 84

Chapter 5
Beings of Heaven 91
   God 92

   Angels 98

   Ghilman 102

   Houris 103

   Animals 108

   Jinn and Extraterrestrials 111

Chapter 6
Entering Heaven 113
    Settling Scores...................... 117
    Cistern of Kauthar 118
    The Gates of Heaven 122
    Our Altered Psyche 128
    Our Bodies......................... 132
    Clothes............................ 140
    Collecting Outside the Gates......... 142
    Entering the Gates 144
    Transportation to Heaven 146
    The Welcome Banquet................ 150
    Death of Death 156
    Transportation to Your New Home..... 157

Chapter 7
What You Will Get in Heaven 159
    The Last Person to Enter Heaven....... 161
    Territory 167
    Mansions........................... 169
    Marriage and Sex 175
    Servants 183
    Food 183
    Drinks 187
    Rivers of Heaven 189
    Geography of Heaven 191
    Weather............................ 197

Time. 198
Interests and Passions 200
Fragrance of Heaven. 202
Socializing with Friends and Relatives. . 203
Music and Entertainment 207
Language of Heaven. 212

Chapter 8
Meeting God—
The Ultimate Experience 215

Chapter 9
Shopping Malls of Heaven. 227
Clothing. 231
Jewelry. 233
Perfumes 234
Other Goods 235
Vehicles. 237
Public Square and Meeting People 240
Restaurants and Bars 241
Museums, Art Galleries, and Libraries. . 244
Home Again 246

Chapter 10
What Heaven Will Not Have 249
Boredom. 256
Sadness 258

Chapter 11
How to Go to Heaven 261
- Minimum Requirement—
  Belief in One God................... 268
- Relationship with God 271
- Asking for Forgiveness.............. 272
- Being Grateful...................... 274
- Fulfilling Religious Obligations...... 275
- Beliefs 276
- Obligations to God 279
- Obligations to Mankind............. 282
- The Points System 286
- Satan's Challenge to God............ 296
- Satan's Method of Attack 298
- Advice for Christians............... 301
- Intercession 306
- Summary of How to Get into Heaven.. 309

Chapter 12
Conclusion 311

Endnotes 321

Bibliography 333

Preface

Like many people, I have pondered over the reason for our existence and the meaning of life and have arrived at what I believe to be a satisfactory answer. In my view, the answer lies in teachings about the afterlife as taught by Christianity and Islam, and I would like to share my findings with you in this book.

Let us consider that everything we do in this life is usually done with a goal in mind. We are likely to know what our goal is, and we make an effort towards achieving it. Surely the most important goal we should all have is to fulfill our life's purpose. But what if the whole purpose of life on this earth were to gain entry into heaven? Most of us have only a vague idea of what heaven will be like, so how can we do what is necessary to go there? This book offers a detailed description of heaven, and it is my hope that the information provided here will motivate us to do what is required to be admitted into it.

A major objective for me in writing this book is to share my knowledge with my sons, nieces, nephews, and other family members. In addition, I hope that the book will reach young people everywhere, as well as everyone who is seeking a meaning for their lives.

Relevant quotations from the Qur'an are used throughout the text, and the chapter and verse numbers are provided in parentheses; e.g., "(2:20)" refers to chapter 2, verse 20. The translation of the Qur'an that I have used is by M. A. S. Abdel Haleem, published by Oxford University Press.

Introduction

Do you believe in heaven? Have you ever wondered what it might be like? Will it be a physical place or a spiritual one? Will there be houses in heaven? Will we eat and drink? Will we go shopping? These are the questions I've often asked myself. In this book, I will provide precise answers to these questions and give the reader a more detailed description of heaven than has been available previously.

Having been raised Muslim, I have drawn from both traditional and less well known Islamic sources. Islamic texts give fairly detailed descriptions of heaven, but even many Muslims are unaware of this information, including myself until not very long ago. Although this knowledge has been available for over a thousand years, I never knew many of the details about the afterlife until I began delving deeper into the subject.

The information I uncovered creates such a vivid picture of heaven that it has forever changed my own view of life. Now this world doesn't seem so important anymore, and my goal in life is to go to heaven and to share this information with others so that they, too, can go to heaven. Isn't this what all the prophets tried to do? They believed in God and the afterlife, and they tried their best to tell people about it.

I've been interested in the subject of life after death for a long time and have been aware of many of the details from Islamic teachings, but the overall picture was still fairly vague in my mind. Very often, while walking around in nice shopping malls, I would ask myself whether there could be something similar to these in heaven. Shopping malls are pleasant places, with beautifully decorated stores and well-dressed people. It occurred to me that maybe in heaven there might be public places where good-looking people in gorgeous clothes would be walking around among shops, restaurants, and beautiful surroundings. Then one day, I happened to be watching a video about a tradition of Prophet Muhammad, and it described how residents of heaven will have a meeting with God, and afterward they will visit a marketplace where they will receive free gifts. That was a moment of epiphany for me, as it answered the question I had been thinking about. There really will be shopping malls in heaven. This thought made the concept of heaven seem much more real to me than it had ever been before. It was as though I had been transported there. I suppose the human desire for material possessions is so strong that it took the promise of free gifts to get my attention. The thought of there being marketplaces in heaven full of wondrous goods inspired me to search for more details.

My subsequent research produced a wealth of information that I had never known to exist. For me, the result is that heaven now feels so real that it seems as though it is ready and waiting for me to arrive there. It's like planning a trip to a beautiful holiday resort—you already have a good idea about what to expect, although the reality is often even better than what you imagined. In fact, the amount of information that we may have about an exotic vacation package before making a booking is likely to be similar to, or less than, what we know about the afterlife as described in Islamic literature.

Most of the details in this book are derived from reliable sources that are easily accessible, but I've also tried to uncover less well-known details and attempted to find all available information on the subject. I believe that I've tapped into all extant knowledge on the subject—although there's always the chance of some tidbits of information being hidden away from view on a dusty library shelf somewhere that I may have missed.

The main and most well known source is the Qur'an, which has many vivid descriptions of heaven—far more than the Bible. Among all Islamic sources, the information in the Qur'an is considered to be the most authentic, as it is believed by Muslims to have been dictated by God himself and is preserved in its original form. I have quoted over two hundred verses from the Qur'an that mention heaven, although there are many more that are repetitions.

The second major source of information consists of various collections of *Hadith*,[1] which are the traditions of Prophet Muhammad describing things he did and said. There are many hadith collections, and I've studied all the major ones. Six of them are considered to be the canonical texts of Islam and include Bukhari, Muslim, Dawood, Tirmidhi, Ibn e Majah, and Al-Nasai. Two others are Ahmed and Malik. All these texts date back to the ninth century, and almost everything written by Islamic scholars after that time is based on these books. I have provided almost two hundred and fifty references from the Hadith.

Beyond that, there are dozens of books written on the subject of heaven, some contemporary and a few from a long time ago. One famous book is called *Hadi al-arwah ila bilad al-arfah* (The Leader of the Souls to the Land of Joy), which was written by a reputable scholar, Ibn Qayyim Al Jawzyya, almost 700 years ago in Damascus.[2] Unfortunately there's no English translation of this book that I know of, and it would be great if someone could translate it.

In addition, there are numerous lectures by scholars available on video sites, such as YouTube, that are a source of many interesting details. I also draw ideas from other Abrahamic religions—Judaism and Christianity—and even New Age beliefs, and from science.

For me, there is no contradiction between religion and science. Religion merely describes the reality that lies beyond the point where science reaches its limit. Heaven, as described here, seems to be an advanced high-tech environment where those things will be a reality that humans are always trying to achieve on earth, such as bodies that don't die, peace and security, and unlimited wealth. Heaven will be a real physical place—maybe it already exists in a parallel universe—and at any given moment in time, we are seconds away from being transported there, because with our last breath, we will find ourselves in a whole new universe.

I hope that people of varying beliefs will derive benefit from this book. If you're already a Muslim, then you have a head start because you already believe in God, resurrection, judgment, and heaven and hell. For you, this book will provide more details.

I am particularly hoping that Christians, whether practicing or not, will read this book. If you're a Christian, then it's likely that you already believe in heaven, so you're a potential beneficiary of the information I present here. According to surveys, more than eighty percent of Americans believe in an afterlife, but various denominations have differing opinions about details such as whether heaven is physical or not. Some churches hold beliefs that can be considered very similar to Islamic ones.

The reason this book will be of great value to even the most dedicated Christian is that the information on the afterlife available in Islamic literature is far more detailed than what is available in Christian eschatology. You will be able to fill in a lot of gaps in your knowledge of heaven, and it will, hopefully, start seeming much more real to you. The best book on the Christian view of heaven is Randy Alcorn's *Heaven*, which I found to be very close to the Islamic viewpoint. If you've read that book, then this one should fill you in with many additional details.

Even if you are not a believer, you should read this book. At the minimum, it will introduce you to a fantastic world that beats anything in science fiction. It reminds me of reading a news item on CNN's website about how some people became depressed and suicidal after watching the movie *Avatar* because they longed to experience the beautiful world, Pandora, depicted in that movie, and they were sad that it's not possible to go there. Heaven, on the other hand, is infinitely better than Pandora and is as real as this world, and it is actually possible to go there. After reading descriptions of all the good things available in heaven, you might even be convinced that it really does exist and you would like to go there.

For those who are already convinced of the existence of heaven and have a desire to go there, I will present you with a roadmap. I will tell you about the minimum requirements for going to heaven—which is to believe in one God. Just as heaven is real, hell is also real, and I will also tell you how to avoid it. Going directly to heaven while avoiding any time in hell is the supreme triumph for man, and I hope to help you achieve that objective.

I would like to add a disclaimer here. I am a layperson, not an Islamic scholar, and this book should be considered my own personal interpretation of Islamic teachings about heaven, not a scholarly work. Even though I have derived all my facts from authentic Islamic sources and provided over four hundred references, I have also added many thoughts of my own.

What I have attempted to do is similar to what paleontologists do when they take fossils from the ground and use them to reconstruct whole dinosaurs. In movies, you can see dinosaurs that look almost real. What they have done is to use bones and fragments to reconstruct complete dinosaur bodies using logic and imagination. They don't just show you skeletons and leave you to imagine the rest of the animal yourself; they make the effort to reconstruct the whole dinosaur and show you the finished product. Similarly, I have used authentic material and added my logic and imagination to paint a more complete picture of heaven. Where there are gaps in the available information, I have filled them with my own speculation. If you were to go back in time and see real dinosaurs, it's likely that you would recognize them because real dinosaurs were probably fairly similar to the ones you see in paintings and movies. I hope that where I've filled in the gaps with my own ideas, the reality will not be too far off.

Significance of the Number Seven

The number seven occurs frequently in various hadiths, especially in the form of seven, seventy, or seventy thousand. This comes from a cultural tradition of the time.

When this number is mentioned, it shouldn't necessarily be taken literally as describing an exact quantity of something; rather it should be understood to mean a lot, as today we might use the number one hundred in a similar context. One technique may be to mentally substitute the number hundred for the number seventy. So, if the Hadith says you'll have seventy of something, you can imagine that you'll have a hundred of that, and when it says seventy thousand, you can think of one hundred thousand.

I

What Is Heaven All About?

Our souls yearn for heaven. Whether one believes in God or not, it is a condition of being human that we all seek security, comfort, beauty, and perfection. It seems to be built into human nature.

What causes our souls to seek perfection? The reason for this can be explained by perusing the story of man's creation as told in the Qur'an and Hadith. We're told that mankind was created to live in a perfect heaven, but then we ended up being downgraded to this less-than-perfect earth. If someone has grown up living a life of luxury and is then reduced to poverty, he will never be at ease and will always yearn for what he's lost, and that's our condition in this world. Our souls were designed to live in a perfect environment, but we've ended up in this imperfect world, and I'll tell you the story of how that transpired.

God himself is intangible and without any material form. He created all of existence, including this universe and perhaps many others. He also created infinitely many kinds of life forms, many of which are intelligent beings, like angels and humans. Some of the intelligent beings, such as angels, do exactly what they're told, like automatons, while there are some that have free will, like humans. There are many inhabited worlds out there in the universe, and one of them is this earth inhabited by us, with the first humans having been Adam and Eve.

Scientists tell us that humans developed through evolution over many millions of years. I believe that it is true that our bodies evolved over millions of years, just as scientists tell us, but the creatures that existed previously were not real humans. They were, for all intents and purposes, animals with a high degree of intelligence but no souls. Since some people believe that animals also have souls, one could say that the early hominids had animal souls, not human ones. At some point in time, a new creature was introduced into this world with a soul, and that creature was Adam, the first human. This happened about ten thousand years ago, which is around the time that civilization began on earth. Although archaeological records exist of humanoids being present tens of thousands of years ago, most traces of settled civilizations don't go back more than around ten thousand years, which is the approximate time of Adam and Eve's arrival on earth.

Many inhabited worlds may have existed on other planets before our time, maybe millions of years ago. Many may exist now all over the universe, and others will exist after we're gone. At some point in time, God decided to create another being with intelligence and free will and test them to see how they would behave. That's where our story begins.

God created Adam from physical matter, as opposed to the angels, who were made from light, and jinn, who were made from fire. "We created man from an essence of clay." (23:12) "Then He molded him; He breathed from His Spirit into him; He gave you hearing, sight, and minds. How seldom you are grateful!" (32:9) After God had created both Adam and Eve, he put them in heaven. "But you and your wife, Adam, live in the Garden. Both of you eat whatever you like, but do not go near this tree or you will become wrongdoers." (7:19)

God created Adam in two stages: first he fashioned his body from physical matter and then blew into him from his own spirit. This is an important point in understanding the difference between body and spirit.

The body is made from physical matter, while the soul is intangible and nonmaterial, created from the spirit of God, blown directly into the body, and humans are made in the image of God.[1]

Being made in the image of God means having characteristics similar to his. The Qur'an lists ninety-nine names of God, each of which is an attribute of his personality, and we're able to understand what they mean because we have a similar nature. For example, *Ar-Rahman* means the compassionate, and humans also have compassion; *Al-Alim* means the knowing, and humans also have knowledge; *Al-Khaliq* means the creator, and humans also like to create things; and so on with almost all the names of God. God may have many more attributes, but the ones we've been informed about are similar to the ones we have.

When Adam and Eve were created, their bodies were not the same as the ones we have on earth, since they were living in heaven, which is in a different universe, and their bodies were perfectly matched to inhabit that environment. Their souls were also different from the ones on earth, optimized for a life in heaven.

Let me say here that the consensus view in Islam is that the Garden of Eden, where Adam and Eve dwelled, was not on this earth, and it was either the same heaven as the one we will be going to, or one similar to it.

Heaven, as we will describe in this book, will be a totally different and perfect environment. The weather in heaven will be different; there will be no sleep, and the food and drinks will be different, and all of these things will require a different kind of body suitable for living in a new world. Therefore, our bodies in heaven will not be the same as the ones we have on earth.

The same is true for a soul living in heaven. Although all souls are created exactly alike, and the same souls we have on earth will be the ones we will have in heaven, there are certain characteristics, or properties of our souls on earth, that will be missing when we're living in heaven; our negative characteristics, such as jealousy, greed, envy, etc., will no longer exist. These traits may help us survive on earth by making us more competitive and providing us with additional motivation to struggle to get ahead, but in heaven, these behaviors will not be required or welcomed and will be eliminated.

We will see later in the book how, before entering heaven, we will be given a drink from a spring that will result in all our negative feelings being switched off.

After Adam and Eve ate the forbidden fruit in heaven, it switched on all the negative characteristics of the soul that they had been shielded from until that time, which also explains why, after eating the fruit, they suddenly became conscious of their nakedness and began to feel ashamed, which is a negative feeling, and started trying to cover their bodies with leaves.

Because our souls are designed to live in heaven, albeit with negative characteristics switched off, when we're living on a vastly inferior planet like earth, our souls yearn for the perfection that only exists in heaven and cannot be found on earth.

Our souls were created from the spirit of God and optimized for living in a perfect body in a perfect environment. Therefore, heaven is the only place where we can ever be fully at peace with ourselves and with our surroundings. When superior souls were put in inferior bodies and made to live on an inferior planet, this resulted in a mismatch, which led to unhappiness and a struggle to replicate heaven on earth, whether by trying to surround themselves with luxury, creating beautiful works of art, wearing beautiful clothes, or walking in a nice garden, etc. All these things are characteristics of heaven, and heaven seems to be so deeply ingrained in our souls that sometimes we get inspired and actually manage to create exquisite artwork that seems to come from another world. I believe that when people create art, they're actually tapping into an innate knowledge of heaven that each of us has deep within our souls.

Our real home, therefore, is heaven, not earth, and the real struggle in this life is to somehow get back to where we really belong. This, then, is the fundamental purpose of life from our point of view, and all our actions are supposed to be directed towards achieving the aim of entering heaven.

It may be asked, "If we were meant to live in heaven, then why did God put us here on earth, and how do we go to heaven?" I will try to answer the former question here, and address the latter one at the end of the book and explain what is required to get into heaven.

Why Did God Create Us?

Why did God create us in the first place? Only by figuring out the purpose of our existence and then doing what we're required to do can we expect to get into heaven.

There are two kinds of intelligent beings: those with free will and those without. Each of these can exist in a material state with physical bodies or in a non-physical state. By "non-physical" I mean non-solid, for angels are made from light; they are composed of some sort of light particles, like photons, which technically have physical properties.

Angels are nonmaterial beings without free will, and Islam also recognizes another category of nonmaterial beings, called jinn, that have free will. Humans are material beings with free will, whereas in heaven we are going to encounter physical, human-like beings, both male and female, without free will.

Before the creation of mankind, there already existed angels and jinn. "We created man out of dried clay formed from dark mud—the jinn We created before, from the fire of scorching wind." (15:26-27) Angels are intelligent and do exactly what they're told without any disobedience, although they do ask questions if they don't understand something. "[Prophet], when your Lord told the angels, 'I am putting a successor on earth,' they said, 'How can You put someone there who will cause damage and bloodshed, when we celebrate Your praise and proclaim Your holiness?' but He said, 'I know things you do not.'" (2:30) Angels ask questions for their own knowledge, but do exactly what they're told, without hesitation.

The above verse from the Qur'an makes it plain that God intended mankind to live on earth because he said, "I am putting a successor on earth." The explanation for that is that God knows the future, and even before creating Adam and Eve, he would have known that they would disobey him and end up being expelled from heaven. If God stopped creating things just because he knows the final outcome of every act of creation, then he would end up creating nothing. He knows the end result of everything, but still allows events to run their course. Despite the fact that mankind was going to live on earth, human souls would have been designed for living in heaven because their sojourn on earth was to be for a short period of time, after which they were to live in heaven for eternity. Souls, once created, do not perish, as I will explain later.

The Qur'an describes how God taught Adam something and then held a competition between Adam and the angels, and Adam won. The advantage Adam had was the power of deductive reasoning, making him more intelligent than the angels. In addition, he had free will, giving him the choice of obeying or disobeying God.

God loves to be appreciated and praised, and an intelligent being that can appreciate, love, and obey God out of choice probably pleases him more than a being who has no independent will and worships God unceasingly, such as an angel.

The immense intelligence of humans and the vast amount of knowledge they are capable of acquiring allows mankind to appreciate God and marvel at his handiwork. A top scientist working on the frontiers of science can appreciate the wonders of the universe and, therefore, be more impressed with God's capabilities. If he then praises God for his creation, it may be worth more than the praise of someone with lesser knowledge.

Jinn and mankind are two beings with free will, and God's purpose for creating them was to worship him:

"I created jinn and mankind only to worship me." (51:56) Angels unceasingly worship God, but he prefers the worship of mankind.

God created us to worship him.

Notice that the Qur'an uses the term "only," meaning that there is no other reason why God created us. It is possible that some people were expecting something more profound and grandiose as the reason for our creation, and they may be disappointed. But the reality is that the central character in all of existence is God, not us.

God created us to worship him, and as a reward for fulfilling that purpose, he has promised us heaven. From our own point of view, our purpose in life is to satisfy God's will for us and to get into heaven. There is no contradiction between wanting to worship God solely to please him, or worshipping him because we want to go to heaven, since both are the same thing. We will only go to heaven if we please God, no matter what our motivation is. The Qur'an is God himself talking to us, and he mentions heaven hundreds of times and says that going to heaven is the ultimate achievement, or the supreme triumph, for mankind: "On the Day when you [Prophet] see the believers, both men and women, with their light streaming out ahead of them and to their right, [they will be told], 'The good news for you today is that there are Gardens graced with flowing streams where you will stay: that is truly the supreme triumph!'" (57:12)

Almost two dozen times in the Qur'an going to heaven is called the supreme triumph for man.[2] If God himself is telling us that going to heaven is the ultimate success that we can achieve, then it can be said that from our own personal point of view—

The purpose of life is to go to heaven.

Whatever we do in this life needs to be with the intent of helping us get into heaven, and, since heaven has many grades, the more effort we make, the higher the grade of heaven into which we will gain entry.

During the time of the Prophet, his companions used to talk about heaven very often, and the desire for going there motivated them to worship God more. In equal measure, they were frightened by descriptions of hell and did whatever they could to avoid it.

Today, knowledge of heaven has slipped from the minds of most people, even practicing Muslims, but the more we know about it, the more motivated we will be to make an effort to gain entry into it.

It is fallacy trying to rise above the desire for heaven and claiming that we worship God only for the love of him. If you serve a king and tell him that you don't care for the gifts he has promised you, then you're likely to offend him. On the other hand, if you tell the king that you await with great expectation the bounties he has promised you, while fulfilling his commands, it will please him, and it will make him happy to see you enjoying his gifts and appreciating his generosity. Similarly, God's pleasure with us will not end when we fulfill our purpose in this life. He will continue to derive enjoyment from seeing us living happily in heaven and appreciating his generosity. We will continue to praise him for the rest of eternity for the gifts we will receive.

In another place, the Qur'an says, "It is He who created the heavens and the earth in six Days—His rule extends over the waters too—so as to test which one of you does best." (11:7) God will chose those of us who, in his view, are the best. The privileges granted to people in heaven will be so vast, including regular meetings with God, that God will only grant them to people who pass the test, and passing the test includes believing in him and also doing good in this world.

Why Did God Remove Us from Heaven?

After creating Adam and Eve, God put them in heaven. Their bodies and souls were perfectly suited for living in that ideal environment of security and luxury, but they carried a liability, and that was that they had free will. However, they wouldn't have had the capacity for negative feelings, such as hate and jealousy, as these are not required or allowed in heaven, but they still had the built-in capability to disobey God.

The second complication was that before Adam's creation, there already existed another kind of intelligent being with free will, the jinn, among whom there were rumblings of discontent, since they feared that man would be more honored in God's eyes than they were.

The jinn are nonmaterial, intelligent beings made from a kind of energy source called *smokeless fire* in the Qur'an. "He created mankind out of dried clay, like pottery, the jinn out of smokeless fire." (55:14)

Jinn are very different from angels; firstly because, unlike angels, they have free will that gives them the capacity to disobey God, and secondly, due to a whole list of other differences. Angels are asexual, while jinn are male and female and procreate. Angels are not put to any test, while jinn are being tested like humans and will be judged and rewarded by being sent to heaven or punished by being sent to hell, as we will be. The jinn are born and they die. They consume nutrition. They feel pleasure and pain. So, essentially jinn are more similar to humans, except that they're nonmaterial in that they don't have solid physical bodies. They are said to be more inclined towards evil than humans, although there are supposed to be good jinn too. Most paranormal activities we encounter that are attributed to demons, ghosts, and poltergeists, are most likely jinn. They have a mischievous streak and love to hoodwink people.

The leader of the jinn was Satan, who, before Adam's creation, was highly honored and was living in the company of angels. Because of his pride in this position of honor, when Satan found out that God was going to create man and give him a status higher than Satan's, he decided to rebel and challenge God with the help of fellow jinn who followed him. God would have known about the brewing rebellion and Satan's disdain for humans, so when he created Adam, he asked all the angels to bow down to Adam, perhaps to expose Satan in front of all those present in the assembly. "We created you, We gave you shape, and then We said to the angels, 'Bow down before Adam,' and they did. But not Iblis: he was not one of those who bowed down. God said, 'What prevented you from bowing down as I had commanded you?' and he said, 'I am better than him: You created me from fire and him from clay.'" (7:11-12)

Iblis is the Arabic name for Lucifer. Before he rebelled, he is referred to in the Qur'an as Iblis, and after his rebellion, he is referred to as Satan.

According to the Quran, Lucifer was a jinn, not an angel: "We said to the angels, 'Bow down before Adam,' and they all bowed down, but not Iblis: he was one of the jinn and he disobeyed his Lord's command." (18:50) Angels do not disobey God, and when told to bow down to Adam, they did it immediately without hesitation, while Lucifer did not.

Satan refused to bow down in front of Adam and argued that he was superior to "the lump of clay," and therefore his ill intentions were exposed and God cursed him and was likely to hurl him and his followers straight into hell, when Satan asked for respite until the Day of Judgment and said that he would lead most humans astray to defeat the purpose of God. God granted him this respite and said that he would fill hell with Satan and those who follow him, both jinn and men, at the same time decreeing that Satan would have no power over the true believers in God.

The Qur'an says, "When we said to the angels, 'Bow down before Adam,' they all bowed down, but not Iblis. He retorted, 'Why should I bow down to someone You have created out of clay?' and [then] said, 'You see this being You have honoured above me? If You reprieve me until the Day of Resurrection, I will lead all but a few of his descendants by the nose.' God said, 'Go away! Hell will be your reward and the reward of any of them that follow you—an ample reward.'" (17:61-63)

Satan said that he would lead most humans astray, and his reason for wanting to do so was out of jealousy and anger and also to show God that human beings were not worthy of being honored above him. While jinn are born and die (they're said to have a lifespan of up to a thousand years), Satan is still alive because of the time he's been granted until the Day of Resurrection. He knows he is going to be punished for his disobedience, and he wants to take as many of us into hell with him as he can.

It seems that when the new creature, Adam, appeared, Satan knew that Adam would be tested and fail and end up living not in heaven but on earth, because he asked for respite until the Day of Resurrection, even though Adam was still living in heaven. It is possible that Satan and the jinn were also living conditionally in heaven as long as they never disobeyed God, which was similar to Adam's mandate, that as long as he always obeyed God, he could continue living in heaven. Otherwise, he would be removed from it. As soon as Satan disobeyed God, he might have expected that he was going to get expelled and would have to live and die on earth, be resurrected, and face God's judgment. He asked to be allowed to live until the last day, while other jinn have limited lives.

A major difference between Adam and Satan was that when Adam disobeyed God, he immediately repented and asked for forgiveness, while Satan did not repent and only asked for time to corrupt Adam and his progeny. It is said that Satan's arrogance is such that he refused to ask God for forgiveness and will not do so until the Day of Judgment, when the period of respite given to him will end, and he will be seized and thrown into the deepest level of hell.

Since they were expelled, the jinn have no more access to God or heaven than humans do. They're born and raised on earth, and perhaps on adjoining planets, and they die here. They are clueless about the existence of God and are seeking the truth as we are, and they adopt different religions. Some believe in God and some do not.[3]

It is also said that, unlike what some people may imagine, Satan and his followers are actually very weak in the universe and can be crushed like an ant any time God wants to do so. They continue to exist because God has given them time, not because they are strong. Satan fears God, but his hatred is reserved for mankind, and his mission is to cause as much damage as possible to them. Talking about Satan leading humans to war, the Qur'an says, "Satan made their foul deeds seem fair to them, and said, 'No one will conquer you today, for I will be right beside you,' but when the armies came within sight of one another he turned on his heels, saying, 'This is where I leave you: I see what you do not, and I fear God—God is severe in His punishment.'" (8:48) The Qur'an advises, "You who believe, enter wholeheartedly into submission to God and do not follow in Satan's footsteps, for he is your sworn enemy." (2:208)

The next step was to test Adam and Eve to see if they obeyed God or not. The test could only be carried out if they were ordered not to do something, because if nothing is forbidden, then there cannot be a test of obedience. "But you and your wife, Adam, live in the Garden. Both of you eat whatever you like, but do not go near this tree or you will become wrongdoers." (7:19) God also warned them about Satan. "So We said, 'Adam, this is your enemy, yours and your wife's: do not let him drive you out of the garden and make you miserable. In the Garden you will never go hungry, feel naked, be thirsty, or suffer the heat of the sun.'" (20:117-118)

Adam and Eve were warned that if they disobeyed God, they would be expelled from heaven and become mortal, which is why God told Adam not to let Satan drive them out. If they had passed the test and not disobeyed God, then it could be that all of us would be living a life of ease in heaven and would not have had to go through the tedious exercise of living in this flawed world.

Satan studied Adam and Eve for a while and discovered their weak points and then offered to help them out of their dilemma of having the threat of expulsion hanging over their heads. "But Satan whispered to Adam, saying 'Adam, shall I show you the tree of immortality and power that never decays?' and they both ate from it. They became conscious of their nakedness and began to cover themselves with leaves from the garden. Adam disobeyed his Lord and was led astray—later his Lord brought him close, accepted his repentance, and guided him—God said, 'Get out of the garden as each other's enemy.'" (20:120-123) "Each other" refers to mankind and jinn, as both were evicted from heaven and sent to earth—two types of beings with free will expelled from heaven together.

In another place, the Qur'an says, "Satan whispered to them so as to expose their nakedness, which had been hidden from them: he said, 'Your Lord only forbade you this tree to prevent you becoming angels or immortals,' and he swore to them, 'I am giving you sincere advice'—he lured them with lies." (7:20-22)

Once Adam and Eve had disobeyed God, their souls experienced a change as negativity entered into them, and they were not fit to live in heaven anymore, because they now had the capacity to do the full range of good and evil, something that could not be allowed in heaven. It seems that Satan knew that disobeying God and eating the fruit would remove the block on negative thinking from the souls of Adam and Eve, which is why the Qur'an says, "Satan whispered to them so as the expose their nakedness, which had been hidden from them."

The way Satan communicated with Adam and Eve was the same way he inserts thoughts into our own brains, by whispering them into our subconscious minds like a hypnotist enters suggestions into a person's head. He wasn't necessarily visible to them. We might imagine that we've thought of some idea ourselves, but it could have been inserted into our minds by an external influence. Subliminal messaging is recognized by science as a way of inserting thoughts into a person's mind without their being aware of it.

Regarding Adam and Eve's disobedience, think of it this way: If someone is staying in a very expensive luxury resort, and they misbehave, then it's likely that they'll be asked to leave. Heaven is an advanced and very futuristic environment where you don't have to work for a living and are provided with everything you ask for from your wildest fantasies. It's easy to imagine humans like us living there and creating bloodshed and havoc. In heaven, God gives people whatever they ask for, and we could have been asking for ever more powerful weapons. "Please God, there's a guy I don't like; may I have the latest planet-buster missiles so that I can nuke him?" I don't blame God for wanting to expel us from there.

Unfortunately, only a certain fraction of us are ever going to make it back into heaven. The test is real, and only those who pass it will be allowed in. We've been told that every single human being has been allocated space in heaven, and the share of those who do not enter it will be redistributed among those who do.[4]

Is Heaven Physical or Spiritual?

I would like to clarify right at the beginning that, from the Islamic point of view, heaven is a physical place and not an intangible, spiritual one with disembodied spirits floating around. Among Muslims, there is usually little doubt about the physical nature of heaven. Especially among scholars and clergymen, there is consensus on the subject. It is taken for granted and not discussed very often. There are, however, some who may not be so sure.

In Christian theology, there is much more uncertainty about this question, and therefore even many clergymen are unsure of it. According to Randy Alcorn, author of *Heaven*, he has had debates with priests on the subject, and some of them insist that heaven is a spiritual place, not a physical one.

The reason for Muslims' certainty about heaven being a physical location is that the Qur'an has many descriptions of heaven, and almost all of them are of physical objects, such as flowing rivers, being served cups of wine, eating food, wearing clothes and jewelry, living in houses, etc. For example, one verse says, "They will enter lasting Gardens where they will be adorned with bracelets of gold and pearls, where they will wear silk garments." (35:33) If you exist in spiritual form, you can't be wearing clothes and jewelry.

The Qur'an is a mixture of statements that are clear in their meaning and some that are allegorical. Most references to heaven and hell fall into the category of being literal and not allegorical. Therefore, when the Qur'an says that in heaven, we will be given a wine to drink that will not give us a headache nor make us drunk, then that is exactly what we can expect. "A drink will be passed round among them from a flowing spring: white, delicious to those who taste it, causing no headiness or intoxication." (37:45-47) As we will see, the concept of drinking an alcoholic drink that does not cause headaches or drunkenness follows a general theme in heaven, where everything that we enjoy in this world is carried over, but with its negative side effects removed.

God created humans right from the start with physical bodies. First, Adam's body was created, and then, God blew his spirit into him and he became a human when both body and soul were united. Even without a body, a soul can be conscious, like in dreams, but that is not its natural state. It is designed and optimized to operate within a physical body.

In the Hadith, descriptions of heaven are also very much of physical objects, including relatively detailed descriptions of our bodies. Therefore, anyone having doubts about whether heaven is physical or not should cast them aside and rest assured in the knowledge that we will have physical bodies and will be living in a world of solid physical objects and structures.

Human Psyche

Humans are made of two things—the body and the soul. The body is a physical entity made from biological matter, while the soul is a spiritual entity made from an unknown substance. Even God declined to tell the Prophet about its reality: "[Prophet], they ask you about the Spirit. Say, 'The Spirit is part of my Lord's domain. You have only been given a little knowledge.'" (17:85)

A human being comes into existence when the body and soul are combined. The soul gives us faculties such as consciousness, intellect, moral discernment, and so on.

When body and soul come together, they combine to create something called a *nafs*, which is Arabic for psyche, which governs our behavior.

The psyche is a combination of our animal nature that we get from our biological bodies and a spiritual nature that we get from our souls. Our psyche governs our behavior, and it has to deal with the demands of both the body and soul. When the body is hungry, it has to be fed, and when the soul is hungry, it has to be satisfied too, either by worshipping God or by listening to music or whatever it desires.

It would be wrong to blame all our wrongdoings on our bodies and declare our souls to be innocent, because a soul can also have negative inclinations, such as pride and so on. The Qur'an mentions the prophet Joseph saying, "I do not pretend to be blameless, for man's very soul incites him to evil unless my Lord shows mercy: He is the most forgiving, most merciful." (12:53)

As we will learn later, both our bodies and souls will be different once we go to heaven. Our challenge in this world is to control our negative tendencies and to develop the positive side of our nature.

2

The Period between Life and Afterlife

Here I will discuss what happens after we die, right up to the time we will come back to life again on the Day of Resurrection.

One prerequisite for going to heaven is that we have to die first. Because so many people fear death and consider any mention of it to be an unpleasant subject, talking too much about death may take all the fun out of thinking about heaven. Being afraid of death and having a desire for self-preservation are natural instincts that are necessary for the survival of the human race, but if our minds can acknowledge the existence of the afterlife, then we can rise above the fear of death and maybe even start looking forward to it as a doorway to heaven.

Think of death as being similar to going on a roller coaster ride. You know it is safe and you will be okay, but you are still afraid. Similarly, you can be scared of dying, but you can think of it as being just another adventure from which you are going to emerge on the other side, alive and well.

As mentioned earlier, we are made of two things—our bodies and our souls. Our bodies die and cease to exist, but our souls remain intact forever, and it is our souls that make up who we really are. It is the soul that carries our consciousness, our personality, our memories, etc. Our souls existed before we were born and will continue to exist after we die, and we will be brought back to life in a new body on the Day of Resurrection. People going to heaven will be happy at their continued existence, and people going to hell will wish they had ceased to exist, but annihilation is not an option for anyone, whether they like it or not.

Our souls are made of a substance other than matter that has been created directly from the spirit of God. Once created, a soul will never be annihilated, although it will suffer death. Annihilation of a soul is different from death, and I will explain what that means.

Annihilation of a soul means that it ceases to exist, but once souls have been created, they will never be destroyed. Human souls were nonexistent at some time in the past, but then at a particular moment in time, God created all human souls simultaneously, around the time of Adam's creation, and spoke to them. The Qur'an says, "[Prophet], when your Lord took out the offspring from the loins of the Children of Adam and made them bear witness about themselves, He said, 'Am I not your Lord?' and they replied, 'Yes, we bear witness.' So you cannot say on the Day of Resurrection, 'We were not aware of this.'" (7:172) God was speaking to the souls of all the humans who will ever be born. After creating them, God took a pledge from them to accept him as their lord and they did so, and belief in God was ingrained into our subconscious minds. This explains why all humans have a natural inclination towards believing in God.

Once souls had been created, but not yet born, they were in a state of death. Death means that a soul exists but is not living in a physical body, which is a requirement for being alive. A soul that has never been created is nonexistent, but a soul that has been created but not yet born, exists but is dead; souls of people who have died are also dead, waiting for resurrection. So, there are two types of dead souls—those that have not yet been born, and those that have already lived their lives and have died.

A soul in a state of death, not alive in a body, can still be conscious or unconscious. When the Qur'an says that God talked to human souls and they replied, then that means that they, including each one of us, must have been fully conscious at that time. Although we don't remember it, we were having a conversation with God, but we were still dead based on our definition of death. Therefore, the implication is that souls of people who have not yet been born have experienced a fully conscious interaction with God, and perhaps even with other beings. This memory would have been saved in our subconscious minds, but we may not remember it, just as we may have forgotten something that happened only a few days ago. Forgetting an event does not mean that it never occurred.

Similarly, after death, when our souls will have left the body, we will be fully conscious for a while.

The Qur'an says, "Exalted is He who holds all control in His hands; who has power over all things; who created death and life to test you [people] and reveal which of you does best—He is the Mighty, the Forgiving." (67:1-2) When God says that he created death, it means that death is not nothing; it is something that has been created. What it means is that a soul has been created, and it is present someplace where it may be unconscious or conscious, but it is not in a body.

Think of being dead or alive as being similar to having a Facebook profile. As soon as you register on Facebook, your information comes into existence on Facebook's servers, but without an active profile, you're not alive yet. Your state is like having a soul that has been created but has not yet been born. Then, when you create an active profile and populate it with friends and start posting information, it is similar to being born and being alive. Then, let's say that one day you run afoul of some Facebook policy and they deactivate your account. That's like being dead. You can't interact with people anymore, but all your information is still stored on Facebook's servers and will never be deleted. Then, after some time, they may reactivate your account, which would be similar to being resurrected again on the Day of Judgment. Just as Facebook saves your information, even things you thought you had deleted, God is saving all the information about your life in some vast database located in the Throne of God. More details are provided about the Throne of God in Chapter 4, and, as we will see, it is not a chair but a potentially vast structure.

According to the Qur'an, humans will experience both life and death twice. The first death is the period before birth, when souls are in a state of unconscious death; remember you can also be in a state of conscious death. During the period prior to birth, souls exist but they are not living in a body, and that is the current state of the souls of all the people yet to be born. Then, we are born and become alive with full consciousness, although when we sleep, we are in a state of unconsciousness, but we are still alive.

When we die, that will be our second death, and, as we will see, we will experience both states of consciousness and unconsciousness after our death, meaning that we will be fully conscious for a while, and next, we will be put into a state of deep, unconscious sleep until the Day of Resurrection. Finally, we will be resurrected with new bodies and will experience our second and final life, and there will be no more death, whether we go to heaven or hell.

According to the Qur'an, on the Day of Resurrection, "They will say, 'Our Lord, twice You have caused us to be lifeless and twice You have brought us to life. Now we recognize our sins. Is there any way out?'" (40:11) Life, therefore, means that a soul is inside the body, and lifelessness, or death, means that the soul is outside the body.

Every human will experience two lives and two deaths. All of us have already experienced our first, pre-birth, death, and we are now living our first life. We have yet to experience our second death, and sometime in the future, we will be resurrected to live our second life in heaven.

Once in heaven, we will be alive and fully conscious and will never fall into a state of unconsciousness, meaning that we will not die again, and we will not sleep, either, as the sleep state has been described as the brother of death. There will be no sleep in heaven.[1]

Sleep

Understanding what happens when we sleep goes some way towards understanding what happens after death. The Prophet described sleep as the brother of death, and the Qur'an tells us that our souls are taken away when we are asleep. "It is He who calls your souls back by night, knowing what you have done by day, then raises you up again in the daytime until your fixed term is fulfilled. It is to Him that you will return in the end, and He will tell you what you have done." (6:60) "God takes the souls of the dead and the souls of the living while they sleep—He keeps hold of those whose death He has ordained and sends the others back until their appointed time—there truly are signs in this for those who reflect." (39:42)

During sleep, our soul has left the body and is in a different dimension, which is the same place where souls of dead people go, and this is also the same place where those peoples' souls go who have near-death experiences or are traveling in the astral plane.

Most of the time when we're asleep, we're not conscious, but sometimes we could be dreaming, which is a state of mild consciousness, or we could have a lucid dream, which is a higher degree of consciousness. The point to note is that our soul has separated from the body, but is in a state of consciousness.

Talking about sleep, though not related to heaven, I would like to mention that according to Islamic teachings, dreams can definitely be true premonitions of future events, if interpreted correctly. The Qur'an and Bible both tell the story of Joseph, which revolves around his ability to interpret dreams, thus confirming that dreams can be true. The Prophet said that dreams are a small fraction of the same ability that prophets have to predict future events.[2]

The Barrier

There is a concept in Islamic teachings termed *barzakh*, which means "barrier" in Arabic and is generally taken to refer to the disembodied condition of the soul after death and before resurrection. Descriptions in Islamic literature of barzakh are very similar to accounts of near-death experiences (NDEs) and astral travel, and Sufis, followers of a mystical branch of Islam, consider all these experiences to be related. People who have NDEs often report seeing a threshold that they never cross, from where, if they had crossed, they would not have been able to return. The domain beyond that barrier is what the word barzakh refers to, but it is often used to refer to the whole experience of death. "When death comes to one of them, he cries, 'My Lord, let me return so as to make amends for the things I neglected.' Never! This will not go beyond his words: a barrier stands behind such people until the very Day they are resurrected." (23:99-100) The barrier mentioned here is the threshold from where, once you cross, you cannot come back.

The Qur'an, which is the most authentic source of Islamic theology, has relatively little information about the period between death and resurrection, maybe because it is not so important in the overall scheme of things. It only indirectly refers to the sleep state and says that people will wake up on the Day of Resurrection thinking they have slept for a little while. "On the Day the Hour comes, the guilty will swear they lingered no more than an hour—they have always been deluded—but those endowed with knowledge and faith will say, 'In accordance with God's decree, you actually lingered till the Day of Resurrection: this is the Day of Resurrection, yet you did not know.'" (30:55-56)

In the above verse, the Qur'an makes it pretty clear that people will wake up on the Day of Resurrection thinking that they have slept for less than an hour. In that case, whatever interim experience they will have had between dying and waking up in a new physical body will seem like no more than a dream.

The Prophet's teachings in the Hadith mention various experiences of the dead soul, namely proximity to the body, meeting with angels, and being put to sleep, without giving a precise order in which these experiences will occur. The information is enough to surmise that there is a period of time when the dead person's soul is conscious and has a positive or negative experience depending on whether they have led a good life or a sinful one.

Various sayings of the Prophet refer to different experiences after death, and some scholars have put these in sequential order based on their understanding. According to their interpretations of these sayings, in the first stage, upon death, the soul is met by two angels and taken to heaven, crossing various levels until it reaches the Throne of God[3] and has a brief meeting with him. In the second stage, the soul is returned to the body, where it becomes aware of the body's being prepared for burial and actually being buried.[4] In the third stage, it is approached in the grave by two angels, named Munkar and Nakir, and questioned about its belief in God and, depending on the answer, shown its place in heaven or hell.[5] Those who do not answer the questions correctly are punished.[6] Then, in the fourth stage, the soul is told to go to sleep.[7]

My own interpretation of the sequence of events after death is a little different. In my view, not all people will have exactly the same experience. It will vary from person to person. But before I get into the details, I would like to mention that good people do not need to worry about it because the whole experience will be pleasant and of relatively short duration for them.

In the first stage of death, they could find themselves outside their body, or even inside it, as happens during sleep paralysis. They may be aware of their relatives grieving and their bodies being prepared for burial, and might even witness their own burial. Although the Prophet did mention that a dead person hears the footsteps of people leaving after burial, it is not necessary that everyone will experience this. Some souls might linger in this state for longer than others, while some may avoid this experience altogether. For a good person, being in this condition will not be unpleasant at all, as has been confirmed by people who have had near-death experiences.

The second stage, which happens to everyone, is when two angels take the souls to heaven. The angels ask them about their belief in God and what they did in life, and they might even be taken into the presence of God for a brief meeting. Then, if they are good souls, they are shown visions of their final home in heaven; or, if they are bad souls, then they are shown visions of their final home in hell.[8] They are told, "This will be your abode when God resurrects you on the Day of Resurrection."

In the third and final stage, they are put in a state of sleep and their souls are stored away in barzakh. The next thing they will experience will be waking up on the Day of Resurrection, when it will seem to them as though they have just woken up after a few hours of sleep from the moment of death. The post-death experience will just seem like a dream they had.

Being conscious for a while after death is not considered living, since our souls are designed to live in physical bodies. Once a person is dead, their record of deeds is sealed, and there is nothing they can do anymore to improve their situation in terms of their standing with God on the Day of Judgment. Believing in God or asking for forgiveness after death will be futile. There are, however, things people still alive can do for their dead relatives that will benefit them, such as praying for them and giving charity on their behalf.

There is an exception to the rule regarding the after-death experience of three categories of people. They are prophets, martyrs, and children.[9] These three types of people are taken to heaven straight away and given some sort of temporary bodies and continue to live.

Martyrs are those who have died in the cause of God, and they have been promised several special favors, two of which are that all their sins will be forgiven, and they will be exempt from questioning on the Day of Judgment. In addition, they will be kept alive in heaven in temporary bodies. "[Prophet], do not think of those who have been killed in God's way as dead. They are alive with their Lord, well provided for, happy with what God has given them of His favor; rejoicing that for those they have left behind who have yet to join them there is no fear, nor will they grieve; [rejoicing] in God's blessing and favor, and that God will not let the reward of the believers be lost." (3:169-171)

The Prophet said that martyrs' souls are in green birds that are free to roam in heaven, eating its fruits and drinking from its rivers; and they are able to have conversations with God.[10] I'm not sure what it means for a martyr's soul to be in the body of a green bird, but I presume it is a simplified description of some sort of physical body that is given to martyrs. After the Day of Judgment, martyrs will be given new bodies like everyone else and will go to the highest levels of heaven.

In a commentary on the Qur'an by Ibn e Kathir, he mentions that what the Prophet said was, "The martyrs will be upon the banks of a river by the gates of paradise. Over them will be a green dome. Their sustenance will be brought out to them from paradise, morning and evening."[11] So they will be in a building with a green dome near the gates of heaven, not in the bodies of green birds, but the hadiths about green birds are the most widely known and most often quoted.

Children who die are also kept bodily alive in heaven. They are assigned caretakers who look after them and raise them, and on the Day of Resurrection, they will go to heaven, irrespective of their parents' beliefs.[12] The Prophet mentioned that his toddler son, Ibrahim, who had died, was in heaven being cared for.[13]

There is confusion among many people, including both Christians and Muslims and also followers of New Age beliefs, about the period between death and resurrection. They are led to believe that people will continue to live in a spiritual state until the Day of Judgment, either in heaven or in hell. Randy Alcorn calls this intermediate period the "present heaven" and says that people will live there in spiritual form until they are bodily resurrected. Others believe that the disembodied state of existence seen in dreams, NDEs, and visions is the actual heaven. Even some Muslims think that souls stay fully conscious in that state and are continuously blessed or punished until the Day of Resurrection. There are many reasons why this is not the case.

For one thing, there is no confirmation in the Qur'an or Hadith of a long period of life in this interim period, apart from the mention of some post-death experiences and that prophets, martyrs, and children will be given temporary physical bodies and continue to live. The only thing stated in the Qur'an is that, as mentioned earlier, people will wake up on the Day of Judgment thinking that they have slept for a few hours. If they had lived for a long period of time before resurrection, then they should have memories of that period, not of waking up a few moments after death.

Second, humans are optimized to live in physical bodies and not as spirits. Floating around in a disembodied state is not what humans are designed to do.

Third, the time between death and the Day of Resurrection could well be billions of years. We just don't know how long it will be, nor have we been told. Even the Prophet said that he did not know when the Day of Judgment would be,[14] so it may well be a long time away. If the period turned out to be millions or billions of years, that would mean a very long time for souls to be living without bodies.

Fourth, the Hadith talks about the dead soul being shown their final place in heaven or hell, not about actually experiencing heaven or hell. God's judgment will not take place until the Day of Resurrection, so the dead soul has not yet actually been judged, and for it to spend a long period of time in heaven or hell before being judged does not seem fair, nor does it make logical sense.

One companion of the Prophet fell from his horse and died while on a pilgrimage to Mecca. The Prophet commented that he would rise up on the Day of Resurrection chanting the same prayer that he was saying when he fell down.[15] This hadith reinforces the view that the period between death and resurrection will pass quickly, at least for good people.

Therefore, it is important for people to understand that there is no concept of life between death and resurrection, apart from a brief period of consciousness immediately after death.

There is at least one authentic hadith in which the Prophet is reported to have said that when a person dies, the souls of dead people come to meet him and ask him about events in the world.[16] This suggests that dead souls are given temporary consciousness in order to greet recently deceased relatives, and they may also appear in dreams. Even if this happens, it only occurs in a spiritual dimension, not on this earth, and only for brief moments.

Some people ask about ghosts, or contact with dead people by mediums and other such phenomena that seem to suggest that dead people are returning to this world. The explanation for such things is that, assuming something real is happening, it could be jinn impersonating the dead person. Jinn are known to be mischievous and love to cause confusion. What appears to be spirits of dead people may actually be jinn masquerading as ghosts. A soul is totally intangible and immaterial, while angels and jinn are made of some form of energy. A soul by itself cannot materialize or become visible like a ghost, whereas angels or jinn can.

Astral Projection and NDEs

I've been studying out-of-body experiences (OBEs) for over 35 years, ever since, as a teenager, I started spontaneously having OBEs myself. When this phenomenon first started happening, I would feel like I had woken up from sleep and someone was trying to pull me off the bed by my legs. At other times, I would be sleeping and would feel like I had woken up and was floating in the air above the bed. The third type of experience would be when I felt as though I had woken up but was unable to move my body or even open my eyes, no matter how much I tried. These were all very scary experiences, and while having them, I would try my best to wake up, and at the same time, I would say every prayer I could think of.

In those days, there was very little information available on the subject, but I eventually discovered some books on OBEs by Dr. Raymond Moody and others. They talked about many people having similar experiences and their own exploration of the subject by first overcoming their fear and then allowing themselves to travel away from their bodies and trying to explore what was out there.

Over the years, this subject has branched out into two major fields of study based on out-of-body experiences. One is called astral travel, in which practitioners try to induce the experience deliberately and then go exploring to see what they can find. The other category of OBEs consists of near-death experiences, or NDEs, that spontaneously happen to people who suffer a life-threatening injury or illness.

Astral travel, also called astral projection, is now a relatively popular subject, and you can find several books on it in any bookstore, usually kept in the New Age section. With astral travel, your soul leaves the body, but is kept connected to it through what is referred to as the silver cord, which snaps you back into your body any time you want. The difficult part with astral travel is keeping your soul outside rather than coming back. During astral projection, you are in a dimension called the astral plane, and there are several different types of locations you could move around in. To begin with, you could walk away from your body and look back and see yourself asleep on your bed, and you could walk around your own house. Then, you could go outside your house and fly above the streets of your neighborhood and travel to various places and even visit other cities or countries. The last place you could go to is a different dimension, other than earth, where you could encounter other beings, including dead people, angels, or demons. You could have conversations with other beings and even visit fantastic cities with buildings and streets full of people walking about.

Today, you can buy books, watch videos, or even attend classes that teach you how to experience astral projection. There are even YouTube videos with music, called binaural beats, designed to help induce an astral projection. When I was young and had unintentional out-of-body experiences, I used to get scared and force myself to wake up, but now that I've overcome my fear and want to induce a projection, I'm unable to do so no matter how much I try. I do have lucid dreams sometimes, but they're not as vivid or profound as a full-fledged astral projection.

I mention this because there seems to be so much commonality between Islamic descriptions of death, astral travel, and NDEs. It's safe to say that sleep, dreaming, astral projection, near-death experiences, and death are all related to each other.

In recent years, with improving medical treatment, many patients who have recovered from a near-fatal illness or injury have reported having had a near-death experience. Therefore, doctors and scientists started studying this phenomenon in a scientific manner and began keeping records of thousands of such accounts. Many of these are available online, and I've read hundreds of them and have read many books on the subject. Recently, several bestsellers describing near-death experiences have been published, including *Proof of Heaven*, in which Dr. Eben Alexander, a highly qualified neurosurgeon, describes his NDE. Another popular book on the subject is *Heaven Is for Real* by Todd Burpo, about a little boy's NDE, and a movie based on the book has recently been released.

Having studied large numbers of documented NDEs, I have found that, while each experience is unique and not everyone experiences the same events, all the various kinds of experiences can be grouped together into only a few categories. One is where those having the NDE are outside their body looking on as doctors try to revive them, and they can see relatives waiting in nearby rooms. The second is going through a tunnel of light and finding themselves in another dimension. The third is when they encounter angelic beings and/or dead relatives. The fourth is meeting a being of light that they think is God or Jesus. The fifth is going through a life review in the company of angels and then having a discussion with them about it. The sixth is visions of heaven or hell. The seventh is seeing a threshold from which, if they cross it, they cannot return to the world. The eighth type of experience is being told that it isn't their time to die, so they have to go back. There may be other kinds of experiences, but the ones I have mentioned account for the vast bulk of NDEs. Everyone undergoing an NDE has at least some, if not all, of these experiences.

What I find fascinating about NDEs is that, if not exactly the same, they are very similar to Islamic descriptions of after-death events. The Hadith talks about dead people being aware of family and friends grieving, meeting angels and conversing with them, being taken to heaven, being shown visions of heaven or hell, and finally seeing the threshold beyond which return is not possible—barzakh. People who have actually died obviously cross the threshold and never come back, but people having an NDE stop short of crossing the barrier and are returned to their bodies after being told that their time has not yet come.

Most NDEs are positive, but that may be because people with positive NDEs are more likely to report them. But there are also many people who have described very frightening, hellish NDEs. Some people see heaven during their NDEs, while others see hell, corresponding to Islamic teachings saying that people who die are shown their final destination in heaven or hell.

Because of striking similarities with Islamic descriptions of death, I consider NDEs to be pretty much in conformity with Islamic teachings and continue to read about them and would recommend others to do so as well. Islamic texts are ancient, while NDE accounts are very recent and there's a constant stream of new experiences being published; therefore, I study NDEs to give me an idea of what to expect immediately after death.

I would like to caution readers because, with so many people becoming familiar with NDEs, there seems to be an increasing belief that the other world experienced in NDEs is the real heaven or hell and the disembodied NDE experience is pretty much what the afterlife is like. This is a misconception because, as I explained earlier, the state of consciousness after death is brief, and souls end up being put into a state of sleep. People who have had an NDE have never crossed the barrier of death, but had they done so, they would have been put to sleep and will wake up on the Day of Judgment. At that time, they will discover that they have physical bodies and that they will have to face God to be judged, and that the real heaven, or hell, is physical, not spiritual. Heaven will be much more real and far more fantastic than what people get a glimpse of either by astral projections or NDEs.

Mairaj—The Prophet's Astral Journey

I would like to briefly mention an event in the life of Prophet Muhammad that is referred to as the Mairaj. This was an experience he had in which angels took him on a journey from Mecca to Jerusalem, where he met past prophets, including Moses, David, and Jesus, and then, to heaven itself, where he met those same prophets again, conversed with God, and was shown visions of heaven and hell. This experience of the Prophet is considered to be so real and so important among Muslims that the golden-colored Dome of the Rock monument shown in pictures of Jerusalem was built on the spot from where Prophet Muhammad ascended to heaven. The day is still celebrated every year with special prayers and fireworks.

During this experience, the Prophet was accompanied by the angel Gabriel and taken right up to the Throne of God, where he conversed with God and was given the order for the five daily prayers that Muslims are required to perform.

While some Muslims argue that this was a physical journey, some hadiths confirm that it all happened in a dream state and was actually a spiritual journey. If so, it was pretty much the same thing as astral travel. It had three of the classic stages of astral travel, namely walking around the house, flying to another city, and going on a journey to another dimension. So, I would surmise that there's a strong basis in Islam for astral projection.

3

Doomsday and Resurrection

The End of the World

Regarding the end of the world, first of all we need to keep in mind that what we call Doomsday and the Day of Resurrection are two different events. Doomsday is the day when this world will end, and the Day of Resurrection is the time when everyone will be resurrected in order to be judged by God, and these two events will not necessarily happen at the same time.

Furthermore, Doomsday itself can be divided into two episodes. The first one is when all humans alive on earth at the time will die, and the second one is the potentially long period of time during which the earth and the universe will perish. There could be a huge interval of time between the moment when human civilization comes to an end and the time when the universe itself, including the earth, is annihilated, which may be billions of years off.

The Day of Resurrection is also called the Day of Judgment, which refers to the same thing. In translations of the Qur'an, the Arabic word *qiyamah* is sometimes translated as "resurrection" and sometimes "judgment." Both words describe the same event, the day when all humans will be brought back to life and judged by God. Even though it's called a "day," there are hadiths that describe it as lasting the equivalent of fifty thousand years.[1]

According to the Qur'an, "These people have no grasp of God's true measure. On the Day of Resurrection, the whole earth will be in His grip. The heavens will be rolled up in His right hand—Glory be to Him! He is far above the partners they ascribe to Him!—the Trumpet will be sounded, and everyone in the heavens and earth will fall down senseless except those God spares. It will be sounded once again and they will be on their feet, looking on." (39:67-68)

The trumpet will be blown twice by the archangel Israfil (Judeo-Christian, Raphael or Seraphiel), who stands ready at all times waiting for the order. The trumpet is a sound-emitting device that, when blown the first time, will encompass the universe in a rising crescendo of sound that will get louder and louder. First it will cause every living thing to die and will then start annihilating matter. The mountains on earth will turn into dust and fly away and the whole earth will disintegrate; even the stars and galaxies will die and go dark.[2]

Some say that even the angels will die and then God will order Azrael, the angel of death, to take the souls of the archangels Gabriel, Michael, and Israfil, and the four bearers of the Throne, and finally Azrael will take his own soul.[3] Then, the Throne of God itself will be annihilated and nothing will remain except God. "Everything will perish except His Face." (28:88)

Then, God will say: "I am the Compeller! Where are the tyrants? Where are the arrogant?"[4] There will be no one to answer, since no one will exist other than God. This can be compared to rebooting a computer system to get rid of viruses. In this existing universe all kinds of beings with free will have been allowed to roam around imagining themselves to be independent of God, but ultimately, they will all be annihilated, and when a new universe is created, they will be brought back to life under a tight leash, subject to being answerable for their actions.

Then, there will be an interval known only to God, after which he will recreate the Throne and Israfil, who will be ordered to blow the trumpet a second time. A companion reported that the Prophet said that between the two sounds of the trumpet, there will be an interval of forty "something," but he could not remember forty what—seconds or billions of years.[5] Time, in any case, will have no relevance in that situation, since time itself is a creation of God, and he exists outside of it. When everything other than God ceases to exist, time will not exist either.

When the Prophet was asked when Doomsday would occur, his answer was that no one knows except God.[6] "They ask you [Prophet] about the Hour, 'When will it happen?' Say, 'My Lord alone has knowledge of it: He alone will reveal when its time will come, a time that is momentous in both the heavens and earth. All too suddenly it will come upon you.'" (7:187) "Say, 'No one in the heavens or on earth knows the unseen except God.' They do not know when they will be raised from the dead." (27:65)

However, he did describe general conditions in the world at that time, the main one being that humanity will be deeply steeped in sin and not a single person will be alive who will believe in God.[7] Therefore, since billions of people today believe in God, I think it is fair to say that Doomsday is a long way off, and there's little chance of any of us experiencing it in our lifetimes.

When Doomsday will occur is also of little relevance to us because when we die, we will wake up after what will seem like a few hours of sleep and find ourselves at the Day of Resurrection. It can be said that anyone who has died has already experienced the Day of Resurrection because from their perspective, once they died, they woke up a few hours later, even though from our perspective, their souls are in a state of sleep.

Creation of a New Universe

God has promised that he will reproduce creation: "On that Day, We shall roll up the skies as a writer rolls up [his] scrolls. We shall reproduce creation just as We produced it the first time: this is Our binding promise. We shall certainly do all these things." (21:104)

Once the Throne of God has been recreated and the trumpet blows for the second time, the angels will come back to life and a new universe will be created, within which heaven and hell will be contained. There will be new stars and planets, and one of those planets will be where human beings will be resurrected and judgment will take place.

The Prophet told us that there will be a hundred levels in heaven, discussed later, each of which, I believe, may be a galaxy in itself. The highest level of heaven is called *Jannat al-Firdaus*, Garden of Firdaus, which will be located nearest to the Throne of God, and is the largest in size.[8] Inhabitants of Firdaus will be able to see the Throne of God above their heads, as we see the sun, and everything will be illuminated from the light emanating from it.

In the present universe, all heavenly bodies are orbiting around something—the moon orbits around the earth; the earth orbits around the sun; the sun and billions of stars orbit around the center of the Milky Way; and clusters of galaxies rotate around their own axis. If scientists could measure it, it is quite likely they would find that the whole universe rotates around a central axis. Similarly, in heaven, the center of the new universe will be the Throne of God and everything will be rotating around that, including galaxies representing the various levels of heaven.

Resurrection

The resurrection will take place on a planet in the new universe.

According to the Hadith, a piece of the coccyx (tail) bone of every human is preserved, and on the Day of Resurrection, these pieces will be scattered on the land like seeds. It will rain for a long time and people's bodies will grow in the soil, like potatoes grow underground.[9] Then, on a command from God, people's souls will be joined with their bodies, and every single human who has ever lived will come back to life and stand up. "On the Day the Summoner will summon them to a horrific event, eyes downcast, they will come out of their graves like swarming locusts rushing towards the Summoner." (54:6-8)

"A piece of the coccyx bone" refers to the DNA record of every person, which is preserved and will be used to recreate human bodies. This will be mixed with soil and rainwater, and from it, human bodies will be fully recreated under the ground, and when the order comes, they will get up in a confused state, as though they were awakening from a deep slumber, and start walking around naked and scared, talking to each other.

"The Trumpet will be sounded and—lo and behold!—they will rush out to their Lord from their graves. They will say, 'Alas for us! Who has resurrected us from our resting places?'" (36:51-52)

Once people have come back to life, angels will direct them towards a wide, open plain called *Al-Mehshar*, Gathering Place.

It is estimated that one hundred billion people have lived on this planet, and no one knows how many more will be born until the end of time. Therefore, the total number of people being raised on the Day of Resurrection could be hundreds of billions. If every person were to take up a space of one square meter (about ten square feet), two hundred billion people would fit into an area of eight million square kilometers, which is an area smaller than the size of the United States. The land area of the United States is about ten million square kilometers, so even a planet the same size as the earth would be large enough for the resurrection.

According to the Prophet, people will be barefoot, naked and uncircumcised,[10] suggesting that their bodies will be reproduced based on their DNA records and any body modifications, such as circumcision or tattoos, will not carry over to the new bodies. Certain individuals, such as the prophets, will be given clothes, while the rest will remain as they are, and they will face God in that same condition. The Prophet's wife, Aisha, asked him if men and women will look at each other and his reply was, "The situation will be too grave for them to pay attention to that."[11]

These new bodies will be temporary, to be used for the duration of the judgment process, and will likely be more or less similar to our existing ones. Once people have been judged, they will be transported to heaven or hell, where their bodies will be totally transformed depending on where they're going.

The Qur'an describes how people will talk to each other once they come back to life on the Day of Judgment. They will think that they have woken up from an hour of sleep. "On the Day the Hour comes, the guilty will swear they lingered no more than an hour—they have always been deluded—but those endowed with knowledge and faith will say, 'In accordance with God's decree, you actually lingered till the Day of Resurrection: this is the Day of Resurrection, yet you did not know.'" (30:55-56)

The topography of the planet will be different from earth, with a flat, featureless landscape totally devoid of any mountains, hills, valleys, lakes, or oceans. In the Hadith, it is described as a "reddish white land like it's made from fine wheat flour."[12] The Qur'an says, "One day We shall make the mountains move, and you will see the earth as an open plain. We shall gather all people together, leaving no one." (18:47) "One Day—when the earth is turned into another earth, the heavens into another heaven, and people all appear before God, the One, the Overpowering." (14:48) We are told that the sun (likely to be another star) will be very close in comparison to what we're used to on earth; it will be very hot, and people will be sweating profusely.[13] The sun will probably appear much larger because of its proximity to the new planet. Since, as I have mentioned previously, it will rain prior to the resurrection and bodies will grow in the ground, it follows that the planet's geography and climate will be similar to that of earth, with a breathable atmosphere, clouds, rain, and soil that is suitable for organic growth, since human bodies will be growing in it.

The Day of Judgment is described as a very scary and stressful experience, especially for nonbelievers and sinful people. They will be wondering what is going on; because they had no concept of an afterlife, it will be all the more shocking for them.

Even believers and good people will most likely find it an unpleasant experience, but we have been told that good people will be shielded from the worst aspects of the Day of Judgment, and time will appear to pass quickly for them.

People will form into groups based on their associations on earth; worshippers of various gods and idols will collect together, or they will follow those whom they considered to be their leaders, whether prophets, priests, kings, or chieftains and ask for their help.[14]

The length of the Day of Judgment is said to be fifty thousand years. It is not certain how people will spend that length of time, whether they will eat or drink, or perhaps the perception of the passage of time will be different and it won't appear to be as long.

It is possible that people will be resurrected in batches, and as judgment is passed on one group, the next one will be raised up.

Judgment

"There is no one in the heavens or on earth who will not come to the Lord of Mercy as a servant—He has counted them all: He has numbered them exactly—and they will each return to Him on the Day of Resurrection all alone." (19:93-95)

Although we have access to lots of information about the judgment process, I will only mention a few details and skip the rest, so as not to stray too far from the topic of heaven.

Angels will be present, and they will lead everyone to a gathering place where judgment will take place. It is not made clear whether there will be buildings or any other physical structures at the gathering place, but we are told that each person will be taken individually to face God alone and answer for their lives. The Throne of God will be visible and people will communicate with God, although he will be hidden behind a veil.

Before the process of judgment begins, each person's record will be brought out. Angels that accompany each of us all the time are recording everything we do on earth. "Everything they do is noted in their records: every action, great or small, is recorded." (54:52-53)

Two records are kept for every person, one for negative actions and one for positive actions. This combined record will be presented to them, and it will be so detailed that people will be surprised to see that it contains the minutest detail about them, even things they thought were of little or no significance. "The record of their deeds will be laid open and you will see the guilty, dismayed at what they contain, saying, 'Woe to us! What a record this is! It does not leave any deed, small or large, unaccounted for!' They will find everything they ever did laid in front of them: your Lord will not be unjust to anyone." (18:49)

Scales will be set up that will weigh a person's good and bad deeds. "We will set up scales of justice for the Day of Resurrection so that no one can be wronged in the least, and if there should be even the weight of a mustard seed, We shall bring it out—We take excellent account." (21:47)

God will pronounce judgment on people one by one, and the manner in which they will receive their report will be based on the judgment they have received. "Anyone who is given his Record in his right hand will say, 'Here is my Record, read it. I knew I would meet my Reckoning,' and so he will have a pleasant life in a lofty Garden, with clustered fruit within his reach. It will be said, 'Eat and drink to your heart's content as a reward for what you've done in days gone by.' But anyone who's given his Record in his left hand will say, 'If only I had never been given any Record and knew nothing of my Reckoning. How I wish death had been the end of me.'" (69:19-27)

When we say that people will appear before God one by one, it doesn't mean that only one person will be judged at a time, as that could take millions of years. God's omnipresence allows him to talk to many people, or everyone, at the same time; therefore, there may be millions of people being brought in front of God at the same time and it would appear to everyone that they're alone in front of God.

People who get a positive judgment will then gather in a special location, where they will wait to be transported to heaven. But they will have one final hurdle to cross.

As-Sirat—Bridge over Hell

On the way to heaven, every single person, whether bound for heaven or hell, will have to cross a bridge over hell named *As-Sirat*. During the crossing, people destined for hell will fall off into hell, while people destined for heaven will get across very quickly and arrive at the gates of heaven.

The Qur'an says, "We know best who most deserves to burn in Hell—but every single one of you will approach it, a decree from your Lord which must be fulfilled. We shall save the devout and leave the evildoers there on their knees." (19:70-72)

Traveling from the planet of resurrection to the gates of heaven will require crossing the As-Sirat Bridge.

Since the bridge will pass through a zone where hell will be located, the phrase, "Every single one of you will approach it (hell)," is thought to refer to the time when people will be crossing the bridge. Everyone will get a glimpse of hell, and those destined for it will fall into it. Seeing what hell is really like will cause people going to heaven to appreciate it even more.

My own interpretation of the As-Sirat Bridge is that it could be something like a wormhole to be used to transfer people from the planet where resurrection and judgment are to take place to the part of the new universe where heaven will be located.

Wormholes are theoretical tunnels that can connect distant locations within a universe or even different universes and allow travel between two points at speeds faster than light. The types of wormholes that allow travel are called traversable wormholes. The most respected theoretical physicists, including Einstein, have validated the science behind the existence of wormholes, and the types predicted by Einstein are called Einstein–Rosen Bridges.

The Prophet said that everyone would have to cross a bridge that will pass over hell. People who are destined for heaven will cross it very quickly,[15] while those destined for hell will be caught in hooks and thrown into hell. The wormhole's path will pass through an area of the universe where hell will be located, and it will have kinks that will trap bad people and spit them out.

When good people get across the bridge, they will find themselves at the gates of heaven.

Hell

Although this book is about heaven, I would be remiss if I did not mention that hell is just as real as heaven, and many, if not most, people will go there. We have a lot of information about it, almost as much information as we have about heaven, but I'm skipping over it because I think many people will find it upsetting. Today, people, including myself, are more motivated by pleasant thoughts of heaven rather than by the fear of hell, while in the olden days, frightening people with scary images of hell may have been more effective in keeping them on the straight and narrow. I will just mention a few details.

Hell has seven gates and many levels, with the top level being the least painful and the bottom one being the worst. Just as people in heaven will be going to different levels based on their goodness, people in hell will be put into different levels of hell based on the evil they have done. People going to heaven will get beautiful new bodies before entering heaven, and those going to hell will be transformed into hideous forms before being thrown into it.

Some people who like to joke about hell being an interesting place where all the cool people will be found are mistaken. It will actually be such a horrendous place that the Prophet said that if someone was dipped into hell for even a moment, he would experience such excruciating pain that he would forget about any long and pleasant life he may have lived on earth.[16]

On the Day of Resurrection, the time that God has given to Satan will be up, and he will be seized and flung into the bottom of hell, from where he will never emerge.

The prophets whom people followed in their lifetimes will be present during the judgment process, and each will be given a certain number of followers for whom they can intercede. In this way, some people will be saved from hell completely, while others will be sent to hell and taken out later after suffering a period of punishment. Therefore, there will be people in heaven who previously spent some time in hell. Once the last person who is destined to get out of hell has been taken out, its gates will be shut forever, and there will be no escape after that.

There are people who get indignant at the mention of hell and ask why some people might stay there forever. All I can say is that you need only worry about yourself. If someone in this world commits crimes and ends up in jail, would you express your sympathy for them by committing crimes yourself and joining them? If you were really worried about anyone going to hell, the best way to help them would be to show them the way to heaven. In any case, God is just, and I believe that whatever he does will be just, even if some of us fail to understand it.

Some people lose their faith or refuse to believe in God because of hell. They say that if God is merciful, then why would he put anyone in hell? Therefore, they won't believe in any of it. That's like refusing to believe that jails exist. If someone commits a serious crime, they'll still find themselves locked up, whether they believe in jails or not.

As far as God's mercy is concerned, the prophet said that God divided mercy into one hundred parts and kept ninety-nine parts of it for himself and distributed one part among all his creation.[17] At the time of the prophet, people saw a woman running around looking for her lost baby, and when she saw any baby, she would grab it and start hugging it. The Prophet said to his companions, "Do you think that this lady can throw her son into the fire?" They replied, "No." The Prophet then said, "God is more merciful to his slaves than this lady is to her son."[18]

God has far more compassion and mercy than all of his creation combined, but he also has to run that creation in an orderly and just manner, and whatever discipline has to be imposed in order for the universe to function properly, he will do it. In this world, in countries where there is no rule of law, anarchy prevails. If the universe were run in a haphazard manner like that, it would have collapsed a long time ago.

Transfer from Hell into Heaven

The Qur'an mentions a transition zone between heaven and hell holding those people who have been let out of hell but have not yet entered heaven. It will be located in between the two. In the Qur'an, this place is referred to as *Al-A'raf*, "The Heights." We will call it purgatory here, but it should not be confused with the Christian concept of purgatory, which not all churches believe in and those that do, view it as the intermediate state between death and resurrection.

According to the Qur'an, people in heaven, hell, and purgatory will be able to communicate with each other. The people in purgatory will be able to see the people of both heaven and hell, the two of which will be separated by a barrier, and they will be in the middle somewhere: "A barrier divides the two groups with men on its heights recognizing each group by their marks: they will call out to the people of the garden, 'Peace be with you!'—they will not have entered, but they will be hoping, and when their glance falls upon the people of the Fire, they will say, 'Our Lord, do not let us join the evildoers!'" (7:46-47)

This intermediate place will probably be similar to the planet where resurrection will take place, a planet similar to earth, which is neither heaven nor hell. One by one, the people in purgatory will be transferred to heaven. Later in this book, we will tell the story of the last person who will be moved from hell into heaven passing through purgatory. We will also discuss later how people might be able to communicate with each other, but the point to remember is that we are talking about a new universe that will be technically far more advanced than earth, and if we can communicate around the world with our cell phones today, then I'm sure there will be far more sophisticated technology available in heaven, and probably even in hell.

As people will be taken out of hell, they will emerge in a burnt-out state, and before entering heaven, they'll be dipped in the River of Life, where their bodies will be transformed into beautiful new ones of the kind that people in heaven will have.[19] In the beginning, they will be left with an identifying mark, and in heaven, they will be recognized as the "People of Hell."[20] It is said that this mark will be a ring around their necks, like a necklace. Later this mark will be removed and they'll be indistinguishable from anyone else.

4

Properties of Heaven

Later in the book, I will give you a fairly detailed description of what to expect when you enter heaven, but first, let's get a general idea of heaven.

Heaven will be an entire universe, much larger in size than our existing one, with a very different physical structure, and laws of physics that are different from our own.

Size of Heaven

Heaven will be a physical and real place that will not be just a single planet, or a "New Earth," with one or more cities where we will get nice houses or apartments; it will be much more than that. It will be a whole new universe much larger than our existing one. The Qur'an says, "Hurry towards your Lord's forgiveness and a Garden as wide as the heavens and earth prepared for the righteous." (3:133)

According to several hadiths, heaven is at least one hundred times the size of this universe[1] and is so vast that after all humans destined for it will have been allocated their share, there will be so much vacant space left over that it will be used to accommodate beings from hundreds of worlds other than our own.[2] That implies that people from planets other than earth are also destined for the same heaven as we are, and it is also a confirmation of the existence of many other extraterrestrial civilizations in the universe. That is why the Qur'an begins with the words, "Praise belongs to God, Lord of the Worlds." (1:2)

To get an idea of the sort of scale we are talking about, our own galaxy, the Milky Way, has several hundred billion stars like the sun, and there are several hundred billion galaxies in the universe. Just the part of the universe that is visible to us with our current technology, which is only a fraction of the whole universe, is so large that it has more stars than there are grains of sand on earth.

Think of it in this way: the number of all humans that have ever lived since the beginning of time is about one hundred billion, which is much less than the number of galaxies in the universe, so even if every single person who has ever lived were given a galaxy for themselves in this universe, there would still be hundreds of billions of galaxies left over. And heaven will be at least a hundred times bigger than that, so obviously there's no chance of its ever running short of space, or any likelihood of anyone feeling cramped in any way.

The Prophet told us that when people on one level of heaven will look at people living on another level, they will appear to them like stars,[3] implying that people will be living among different planets, stars, or galaxies. When we look at the sky on a starry night, many of the glimmering points of light we see that we think are stars are actually distant galaxies. Therefore, the people on different levels in heaven will be spread out amongst different stars or galaxies all over the vast new universe.

God's creation is enormous, and he has an unlimited capacity for expanding it. The Prophet said that he was told by God that if every single human who had ever lived got up and asked God for everything they wanted, and if all their wishes were granted, it would not reduce God's possessions any more than water in an ocean would be reduced if a needle were dipped into it and pulled out.[4]

Location of Heaven

Since we have been informed that heaven is a universe much larger than our existing one, then it follows that it cannot be accommodated anywhere within our present universe. For that reason, we cannot say that it might be located in a part of our existing universe that is so distant that we cannot see it with our existing technology. Apart from heaven being too big to be contained within the existing universe, there are other reasons why it is reasonable to believe that heaven is located somewhere outside of our present universe.

Many descriptions of heaven suggest that the laws of nature will be different from the ones we are familiar with here. For example, there will be no night-and-day cycle such as we are used to here; instead, there will be perpetual daylight, with the sky lit up at all times with an all-pervasive, ambient light.[5] The light is said to emanate from the Throne of God, which will be located at the center of heaven.[6] This suggests that there is a central source of illumination lighting up all of heaven, and our source of light will not be a star like the sun in our solar system.

Apart from light from the Throne of God, almost everything else in heaven will emit light as well. There are many hadiths that mention people in heaven emitting light, chairs made out of light, jewels that shine brilliantly, and so on. For example, the Prophet said, "If something of paradise which is lesser than a nail is shown, then everything up to the edges of heaven and earth will be illuminated. And if a man of the inhabitants of paradise were to peep at the world and his bracelets were revealed, then they would outshine the light of the sun just as the sun outshines the light of the stars."[7] In heaven, many, if not all, material objects will be made from light and will be a source of illumination.

Our home planet in heaven will have no associated star and will likely be directly orbiting the Throne of God and deriving its light from it. In that case, the light source will not be direction-based, like light here on earth that casts shadows, but rather it will be ambient, flowing from all directions. This way, our home planet may be rotating, but will still be lit up on all sides, because light will be surrounding the planet. The Prophet told us that the ceiling of heaven is the Throne of God, and we would be able to see God's throne.

Every single planet in heaven, along with its inhabitants, might orbit around the same center, therefore the picture it creates in my mind is of a central source of light emanating from the Throne of God with perhaps billions or trillions of planets orbiting around it; and this configuration could be so large that it will be at least a hundred times the size of this entire universe.

This should be enough to surmise that heaven is a totally different universe from our existing one, before even considering all the other bits of information that suggest that laws of nature in heaven will also be very different.

Does Heaven Exist Now or Will It Be Created Later?

If heaven is a different universe, then questions arise about where it is located, and whether it exists now or will be created in the future after this universe has ended.

Before discussing this point further, let me point out that for all practical purposes, it makes little difference whether heaven already exists or will be created later. When we are ready to go there, it will definitely exist, and we will perceive no delay in arriving there, even if it is created sometime in the future. This is because after death, we will be in a state of sleep, during which we will have no perception of time, and when we wake up, we will find that heaven exists and is ready for us. It will not feel very different from going to bed at night and waking up in the morning.

In Islamic eschatology, it is not clear if heaven already exists or will be created after the end of this universe, as there are arguments in favor of both views. If it already exists, it would need to be some kind of parallel universe of the type that scientists talk about, in a different dimension or somewhere out there beyond the limits of this universe.

Some scientists, including the theoretical physicist Michio Kaku, argue in favor of the multiverse theory, which states that our universe is one among a large number of, or infinitely many, universes. According to this theory, many of those other universes are most likely to have physical laws different from our own, and that is also our understanding of heaven, that it will have physical laws different from the ones we experience here.

People who argue, from the theological point of view, in favor of heaven existing right now, cite verses from the Qur'an that mention heaven in the present tense. One of those verses is one that we quoted earlier that says, "Hurry towards your Lord's forgiveness and a Garden as wide as the heavens and earth prepared for the righteous." (3:133) The word "prepared" is taken to imply that it has already been created, but to me it sounds ambiguous because you could say, "Come to my party next Saturday to eat a barbeque prepared especially for you." I am using an English translation of an Arabic quote to make my point, but the idea would be the same in Arabic as well.

Other texts that are quoted to prove that heaven exists now are related to Hadith narrations that state that when someone dies, they are shown visions of their final destination in heaven or hell. In addition, when the Prophet was taken on a heavenly journey, he was shown heaven and hell, with the implication being that heaven and hell must exist for him to have been given a glimpse of them.

The strongest argument for heaven existing now is the story in the Qur'an about the creation of Adam and Eve and their brief sojourn in heaven. "But you and your wife, Adam, live in the Garden. Both of you eat whatever you like, but do not go near this tree or you will become wrongdoers." (7:19)

So at the time of Adam and Eve, either heaven existed or it was some other place that was similar to heaven. There is no definite confirmation in the Qur'an or Hadith of the heaven that Adam and Eve lived in, and the one we will be going to, being the same one. There are some who say that Adam and Eve were actually living in a garden on earth and were expelled from that, but my own view is that they were living in an entirely different location, which could be the same heaven we will go to after death or one similar to it.

My own analysis of the issue of whether heaven exists now is that if a soul can be transported across spatial dimensions to another universe, it could also be taken across temporal dimensions. A spiritual vision of heaven can be a trip across time to a future universe. In that case, when someone is taken on a spiritual journey to heaven, they are traveling into the future to a time when our present universe will have ceased to exist and a new one will already have been created. If heaven exists now, they should be visiting it at a time when the Day of Resurrection has not yet occurred, and therefore, they should find it uninhabited. However, the Prophet was also shown visions of the Day of Judgment and saw people entering though the gates of heaven, and that is obviously something that will be happening in the future, so either he had actually traveled into the future, or was shown visions of the future.

The reason I am inclined towards believing that the new universe where heaven will be located will be created in the future after the end of this universe, is that the Qur'an says, "Do not call out to any other god beside God, for there is no god but Him. Everything will perish except His Face. His is the Judgment and to Him you shall all be brought back." (28:88)

When the Qur'an says, "Everything will perish except His Face," the implication is that the whole of creation will come to an end. That suggests that if heaven currently exists, it will also come to an end because the word "everything" is all-inclusive. This is contrary to other verses of the Qur'an that state that heaven is eternal: "So enter it in peace. This is the Day of everlasting Life." (50:34)

The only way to reconcile the above two verses, one stating that everything will perish except God and the other saying that we will get everlasting life in heaven, is by assuming that the heaven that we are going to will be created after this universe, and everything else will have been annihilated. A new creation will have been brought into existence that will last eternally, and we will have everlasting life in it.

My own conclusion is that this universe will end at some future date and a new one will be created, with different physical laws, and it will be larger, superior to and more durable than this one, able to exist forever, unlike this perishable universe that scientists agree will most likely cease to exist in a few billion years, either by collapsing back into itself or expanding so far out that it will dissipate into oblivion.

Even though I believe that heaven will be created in the future, I still think that it is okay to talk about it as if it exists now because Islamic texts imply that communication is possible between earth and heaven. People are shown visions of heaven when they die, have a near-death experience, or are in a state of sleep. There are hadiths that talk about beings in heaven who are aware of what people are doing on earth. In this book, I sometimes talk about heaven in the present tense and sometimes in the future tense. I believe that both are correct.

Levels of Heaven

Heaven is not a uniform place where everyone will get the same reward, far from it. It has two major divisions, and within these, there are multiple sub-levels, a hundred or more, each one larger than this whole universe. Not only that, but what you will get will also be different from what anyone else gets, even if they're on the same level as you, because your home in heaven will have been custom-built for you.

The Qur'an states that there will be two levels of heaven, and there will be two of each kind, that is, two of the upper level and two of the lower one. "For those who fear [the time when they will] stand before their Lord there are two gardens. Which, then, of your Lord's blessings do you both deny?" (55:46-47) "There are two other gardens below these two. Which, then, of your Lord's blessings do you both deny?" (55:62)

The Prophet mentioned many grades of heaven that will be sub-levels of the two upper and two lower levels. We will call the two main divisions of heaven "levels" and the subdivisions "grades"; therefore, there will be two levels of heaven and a hundred or more grades.

Within the higher level, there will be one grade that will be the absolute highest degree of heaven, nearest to the Throne of God, and it will be called *Jannat al-Firdaus*, Garden of Firdaus.[8] Even within that, there will be one position reserved for only one person who will be the closest to God, called *Al-Wasilah* (the means by which someone can draw near to God), or *Maqam e Mahmood*[9] (the Praised Position). The person in that position will act as a mediator during the judgment process and be granted the right to intercede on behalf of the most number of sinners. The Prophet said that only one person would get that position and asked his followers to pray that he would be the one to get that spot,[10] and advised them to ask God for the Garden of Firdaus for themselves.[11]

At the time of judgment, people will be divided into three main categories: people of the highest rank destined for the upper levels heaven, people of lower standing destined for the lower levels of heaven, and people of hell.

The Qur'an tells us that the upper levels of heaven will have more people from former times and fewer people from latter times, while the lower ones will have many people from both former and latter times.[12] The reason for this may be that in antiquity people used to take the worship of God much more seriously, while today we are too busy with worldly matters to do what is necessary to qualify for the upper levels.

It has not been explained why there will be two of each of the main levels of heaven. My guess is that it is related to the physical structure of heaven which, being a universe much larger than our existing one, will be divided into major substructures, such as galaxies or galaxy clusters, with two of those reserved for the higher levels of heaven and two for the lower ones. The four major divisions of heaven could each be a galaxy cluster, while the grades could be individual galaxies.

Why would such enormous sizes be necessary for heaven, when more than seven billion of us can fit easily on this tiny earth? Because what each person will receive in heaven will be of such enormous scale that people would need to be spread out over the whole universe in order to be accommodated comfortably. Another thing to keep in mind is that a person in the lowest grade of heaven will be getting something beyond our expectation or imagination, and people in higher levels will be getting a whole lot more, which is why heaven will be of a scale vastly greater than this entire universe.

The two upper levels of heavens will contain similar things as the lower ones, but of superior quality. For example, the buildings and eating utensils of the higher level will be made of gold, while those of the lower level will be made of silver.[13] The (nonhuman) women of the higher level are described as resembling rubies and brilliant pearls, while the ones in the lower level are described as good-natured, dark-eyed, beautiful maidens. There will be two flowing springs in the upper levels and two gushing springs in the lower levels. The people in the upper levels will sit on couches upholstered in brocade, while in the lower levels, they'll sit on green cushions and fine carpets. So, everything in the upper levels will be superior in terms of both quantity and quality. The lower levels will be fabulous, but the upper levels will be even better.

Each of the two levels will have numerous grades, the total number of which has been variously described as one hundred or more, each one larger than this universe.

When God created, or will create, heaven, he created a share for every single human who will ever be born, knowing full well that only a small percentage of them will ever claim it. The parts of heaven left unoccupied because some people will be bound for hell will be redistributed among the people who do make it into heaven. Therefore, every single person reading this has a spot in heaven reserved for them. And heaven is not static; it's continuously being upgraded based on your actions.

The Prophet mentioned some one-line prayers that result in a new tree being planted in your home territory in heaven and other prayers that result in a new mansion being built.[14] The extra daily prayers that result in a new mansion being created for you take about ten more minutes than the usual prayers. Therefore your actions here on earth are continuously increasing your possessions in heaven, and your home is being customized for you. The Prophet told us that when we get to heaven, we will recognize our homes there and automatically know our way around them better than we know our houses here on earth. No GPS device will be needed, as the knowledge of our home in heaven will be programmed into our brains. Presumably this refers to the entire territory that we will be getting, not just the house we will be living in.

At the time of judgment, people will be assigned to a particular grade of heaven based on their deeds on earth and standing with God. When people meet in heaven, those on a higher grade will descend to a lower grade, while those on a lower grade will have limited or no access to higher grades.[15]

Families will not be split because of this, and someone who has earned a position on a lower grade will have their status upgraded to the same grade as their family members earning a higher position.[16] It is possible, however, for families to get split if some members don't make it to heaven at all.

There is a story about how Asma, the daughter of the Prophet's closest companion, Abu Baker, was not happy with her husband, Zubair, and wanted to divorce him. Her father advised her to be patient and stay with him because, although Zubair was a bit harsh, he was destined for a high grade in heaven, and Abu Baker wanted his daughter to join her husband there.[17] Zubair was one of the few people who the Prophet had foretold would be going to heaven.

Throne of God

"Your Lord is God who created the heavens and earth in six Days, then established Himself on the Throne, governing everything." (10:3)

It has been mentioned in the Qur'an that on the Day of Judgment, those who enter heaven will be able to see the *Arsh*, Throne of God,[18] the light from which will provide illumination to all of heaven, and the highest grade of heaven, the Garden of Firdaus, will be nearest to the Throne of God. That raises the question: What is the Throne of God?

God himself is immaterial, outside space and time. Everything we know about, see, or experience, such as electrons, atoms, light, space, and time, are creations of God, and he is not made from any of these, but he still controls all of creation through some physical mechanism. That mechanism, I believe, is what the Throne of God is.

The Throne is the interface between God, who is immaterial, and physical creation, whether it consists of one or many universes. It is a physical entity that is the command-and-control center from where God exercises total control over all of creation.

In a hadith, the Prophet said that in the beginning there existed only God and nothing else. First, God created the Throne and then made the laws of nature, and after that, he created the universe. God also made laws governing his own interaction and behavior with his creation and inscribed all of this information into a book that is preserved in the throne.[19] For example, after creating the universe, God wrote, "My mercy overpowers my anger."[20] So the laws of nature that we study in physics classes, such as gravity, speed of light, and even God's own rules for dealing with his creation, are inscribed in a book, or database, that is located in a physical object that we call the Throne of God.

The Throne of God contains something called the *al-Lawh ul-Mahfuz*, the Preserved Tablet, which is like a computer program that runs the whole of creation. In it are written the laws of the universe, and it also contains a database with information on everything that has happened from the beginning of time and also what will happen until the end of time.

The Preserved Tablet is also related to the concept of destiny, because it already contains information about everything that will happen from the beginning until the end of time. Our actions are not controlled by what is already written, but because God knows what we will do in the future, he has already written it down. "No misfortune can happen, either in the earth or in yourselves, that was not set down in writing before We brought it into being—that is easy for God." (57:22) It is called "preserved" because whatever is written in it will never change. Talking about future events being inscribed in the Preserved Tablet, the Prophet said: "The pens are lifted and the pages are dried." [21]

Let us go over the concept of destiny again. We are free to do what we want to. We can also change future events by praying to God. But whatever the end result is of our actions, it is already known and accounted for and written down in the Preserved Tablet. Therefore, we are still responsible for our actions, but at the same time our final destiny is also known and recorded. The Prophet said that whoever is going to heaven and whoever is going to hell is already written down. Destiny is not

God's will overriding human will. It is a record of what people will actually do in the future out of their own free choice.

We don't know the exact mechanism of God's control over the universe, but the Qur'an says, "He is the Originator of the heavens and the earth, and when He decrees something, He says only, 'Be' and it is." (2:117) He has so much control over everything that just saying "be" brings it into existence.

Also, God is aware of everything to the subatomic level. "Not even the weight of a speck of dust in the heavens or earth escapes His knowledge, nor anything smaller or greater. It is all recorded in a clear Record." (34:3) Information about everything happening in the universe is continuously being recorded in the Preserved Tablet that is kept in the Throne, and God can find out the tiniest detail by reading the record. That's the ultimate example of Total Information Awareness. Even as you're reading this book, that information is flowing into the record and God is looking at it, giving you a direct connection with him.

Regarding the Throne, the Qur'an says, "It is God who raised up the heavens with no visible supports and then established Himself on the throne; He has subjected the sun and the moon each to pursue its course for an appointed time; He regulates all things, and makes the revelations clear so that you may be certain of meeting your Lord." (13:2)

The Throne is likely to be made from the same physical matter that everything else is made from: atoms and subatomic particles. Even though the word "throne" brings to mind a chair, such as a king sits on, it is not a chair-shaped object; its shape is unknown and could be anything, maybe a sphere or a cube. God does not reside inside or on the Throne because he is intangible. The Throne runs by his will and he uses it to interact with creation and exercises control over it.

If scientists were ever to discover the primeval origins of creation, they would discover the Throne and find it to be an object from which instructions for running all of creation seem to be flowing. Creation and destruction of matter, space, and time will all seem to occur from commands coming out of this object. If those scientists were able to look inside it, they would see no one there, since God does not have a physical form. The Throne would just appear to be running automatically by itself and be surrounded by angels, if we could see them.

Being a physical object, the Throne is moved about in physical space, or is carried, by angels, and on the Day of Judgment, we will be able to see it. "You [Prophet] will see the angels surrounding the Throne, glorifying their

Lord with praise. True judgment will have been passed between them, and it will be said, 'Praise be to God, the Lord of the Worlds.'" (39:75)

There are two Arabic words in the Qur'an that are translated as "throne." One is *arsh* and the other one is *kursi*. I think the former refers to the actual physical object that is the Throne of God, while, in my view, the latter refers to God's dominion, as in saying, "His throne extends over the heavens and the earth; it does not weary Him to preserve them both." (2:255) Here, the word throne (kursi) really means that God's dominion, or control, extends over the whole universe. There are some who translate kursi as "footstool" and say that it is also a physical object that is much smaller than the throne.

On the Day of Judgment, we will see the Throne of God surrounded by countless angels singing God's praises, with some angels carrying it. Moving a physical object requires force, and the angels will provide that force. The angels carrying the throne are known as *Hamalat al-Arsh*, Bearers of the Throne. Currently the Throne is borne by four angels, but on the Day of Judgment, it will be carried by eight of them. "The angels will be on all sides of it and, on that Day, eight of them will bear the throne of your Lord above them." (69:17)

There is an interesting hadith from secondary sources in which the Prophet is reported to have said that our present universe, which is the first heaven, is like a ring thrown into the desert compared in size to the second heaven. The second heaven is like a ring thrown into the desert compared to the third heaven and so on, until the seventh heaven. The seventh heaven is like a ring in the desert compared to the kursi and that is like a ring in the desert compared to the Throne of God.[22] This suggests that all of creation might be contained within the Throne, like a computer program running inside a computer.

"These people have no grasp of God's true measure. On the Day of Resurrection, the whole earth will be in His grip. The heavens will be rolled up in His right hand—Glory be to Him! He is far above the partners they ascribe to Him." (39:67)

5

Beings of Heaven

On earth, despite our best efforts to detect and communicate with other intelligent life forms, we have not been able to find any, but in heaven, there will be many different kinds of intelligent non-human beings to interact with on a daily basis. In this life, many of us believe in God and angels, although we cannot see them, but in heaven, we will be able to see them and talk to them and, in addition, there will be another category of human-like beings, with the females called *houri* (pronounced "hoori") and males called *ghilman*. There will also be animals, jinn, and possibly extraterrestrials.

God

In our lives on earth, if we are believers, one of the most disappointing things is our inability to interactively communicate with God. In heaven, however, we will be able to see him and talk to him regularly. The central character in heaven will be God, whose presence will be pervasive, and all activity will revolve around him.

The existence of heaven and our chances of going there are totally dependent on God, just as the existence of this earth and our being on it are dependent on him. Therefore, it is important to know who God is and what he wants. In Chapter 11, we will talk about how to go to heaven, but here we will briefly discuss the nature of God, and also our relationship with him in heaven.

The most important thing that God wants us to know about him is not only that he exists, but also that he is one and indivisible. He is outside of time and eternal; he has always existed and always will. He did not have a predecessor who created him, nor does he have any successor. And there is no other being like him anywhere, not even anywhere in another dimension. The Qur'an says, "Say, He is God the One, God the eternal. He begot no one nor was He begotten. No one is comparable to him." (112:1-4)

The thing God dislikes the most is if anyone, or anything, is worshipped alongside God or instead of him, whether it be a human, idol, or anything else. "God does not forgive the joining of partners with Him: anything less than that He forgives to whoever He will, but anyone who joins partners with God has concocted a tremendous sin." (4:48) Just to accept that God exists and that he is the one and only god is enough to gain entry into heaven and after that, if we worship him and do good deeds, it will help us completely avoid spending any time in hell, and will earn us a higher rank in heaven.

God created our souls, and he even knows what is going on deep in our subconscious minds. "We created man—We know what his soul whispers to him: We are closer to him than his jugular vein." (50:16)

All you need to do to draw God's full attention towards yourself is to think of him. "[Prophet], if My servants ask you about Me, I am near. I respond to those who call Me, so let them respond to Me, and believe in Me, so that they may be guided." (2:186)

But God is not visible, nor does he talk to us. God's way of communicating, even with prophets, was through angels, with Gabriel serving as the main messenger. Moses was the only prophet with whom God spoke directly. But when Moses asked to see God, he was not able to do so because the physics of this world makes it impossible for God to become visible. According to the Qur'an, "When Moses came for the appointment, and his Lord spoke to him, he said, 'My Lord, show Yourself to me: let me see You!' He said, 'You will never see Me, but look at that mountain: if it remains standing firm, you will see Me,' and when his Lord revealed Himself to the mountain, He made it crumble: Moses fell down unconscious." (7:143)

No human has, therefore, seen God, not even the prophets, unless it was in a spiritual state, such as people experience in dreams or visions. God's real self is some form of infinite energy, and if he manifests himself on earth, it causes even mountains to shatter and onlookers to be stunned into unconsciousness.

Heaven will have different laws of nature that will allow God to become visible without pulverizing the environment or causing damage to people. And that is another major difference between the physics of this world and heaven.

In heaven, the highest form of pleasure that people will experience will be meeting God, which will happen on a regular basis—at least once a week. People of higher ranks will see him more frequently, with the maximum being twice a day for the highest-ranking people.[1]

A meeting with God is described in Chapter 8. For now, we will say that you will see God with full clarity and converse with him on a one-to-one basis, and you will be able to talk with him about anything you like, including your life in this world or any topic that you are interested in. You will also be able to ask him for anything you want in heaven. Anyone who, while in this world, feels that there might be any shortcomings in heaven should know that God will regularly ask you if there is anything more you would like, and you will be free to request anything that you want.

This is also the blanket answer to almost all questions about heaven. You can have *anything* you want, and if it does not exist, God will create it for you. Since our nature will be much more temperate in heaven, it is unlikely that anyone will ask for anything improper.

The meetings with God will be so profound and fill a person with such a feeling of ecstasy that all they will be able to do after a meeting will be to think about it. It will be a lingering sense of happiness, and everyone will eagerly await the next meeting.

Meeting God will be so enjoyable that it is called the greatest reward in heaven.

Suppose you greatly admire someone in this world—a famous celebrity, such as a top athlete, actor, or musician, or perhaps the most powerful person in the world, like the President of the United States. Now suppose that you were given the opportunity to meet him every week for lunch. Would you refuse? Imagine meeting with the President regularly and talking with him about the whole world and all the latest issues. If that happened to you, most likely your whole life would start revolving around your weekly meetings with him. Also now imagine that every time you meet the President, he asks you if you would like him to do anything for you, so that you could ask him for anything and he would grant it to you from a special budget reserved for this purpose. If you want a new car, just tell the president and he'll buy you one. Want to go on a vacation? He'll send Air Force One to take you.

God is infinitely more powerful than a president. He has created the whole universe and has absolute power over everything, as well as an endless capacity to create new things. You could ask him to explain the deepest mysteries and he will be able to do that, or you could ask him for a new planet and he could create it for you.

There is another very logical reason why our sense of well-being will peak in the presence of God. That is because God himself has designed it to be so and he has created our souls to derive maximum pleasure from being in his presence.

Engineers design products for specific jobs. Let's say they design a wire for an electrical current of a certain capacity to pass through. If they are producing a wire to carry a high-voltage current, like with wires on an overhead power line, then they will make the wire thicker and stronger and use better-quality materials. If they pass a low voltage current through a high-capacity wire, it will still go through, but the wire's full capacity will not be utilized. But if they pass a high-voltage electrical current, then the wire's maximum capacity will be fully used.

In the case of our souls, God has designed them to be able to experience happiness, but he has made them in such a way that the highest amount of happiness that a soul can ever experience will be felt in his own presence. Being the designer of our souls, he has made them such that our souls will experience maximum happiness when we see him. Every other sort of happiness we experience is only utilizing a partial capacity of our souls for happiness, but in the presence of God, the full capacity of our souls for happiness will be reached. It is a built-in feature.

In heaven, people will be constantly aware of God and praise him with every breath, but there will be no organized worship. There will be no temples or formal prayers, such as the five daily prayers in Islam or Sunday worship in Christianity. People will not be required, or even allowed, to bow down in worship, even though in this life we are strongly urged to do so. The reason for that is that this life is a test for us to see who submits his will to God's. Once we die, the test is over, and in heaven, we will be guests of God and will not be required to do anything to earn any reward. All gifts will flow from God towards us, and we will be constantly grateful to him and praise him, but he will no longer expect us to worship him.

The weekly meetings with God will be the substitute for formal prayers.

Later in the book, we will talk extensively about the material properties of heaven and all the physical pleasures we will experience, but let there be no doubt that the main attraction of heaven, and the source of our greatest happiness, will be our relationship with God. This relationship will be far more profound than anything we can ever experience in this world because we will be able to see God and have conversations with him, and all the material luxuries of heaven will pale into insignificance compared to the pleasure we will derive from our interaction with God.

Angels

Angels are intelligent, sentient beings made out of light.[2] They have no free will and do exactly what God orders them to do. There is a hierarchy among them, with higher-ranking angels being in command of others, and they work to fulfill, without fail, whatever task they have been assigned. In this world, we cannot see angels, but in heaven, we will.

In this life, we are surrounded by angels without perceiving them. There are always two angels with every person, constantly recording their activities. One angel keeps a record of a person's good deeds, and the other one records his or her bad deeds, and this is the record that will be presented to everyone on the Day of Judgment. "We created man—We know what his soul whispers to him: We are closer to him than his jugular vein—with two receptors [usually taken to mean 'recording angels'] set to record, one on his right side and one on his left: he does not utter a single word without an ever-present watcher." (50:16-18) This record will be presented to each person at the time of judgment.

There are always guardian angels with every person: "Each person has guardian angels before him and behind, watching over him by God's command." (13:11)

So, recording angels are to the right and left of every person, and guardian angels are in the front and back. This means that at least four angels accompany each person all the time.

"As for those who say, 'Our Lord is God,' and take the straight path towards Him, the angels come down to them and say, 'Have no fear or grief, but rejoice in the good news of Paradise, which you have been promised. We are your allies in this world and in the world to come, where you will have everything you desire and ask for as a welcoming gift from the Most Forgiving, Most Merciful One.'" (41:30-32)

Each human has guardian angels, but they act as allies especially for those who believe in God and do good deeds. We may never know that they are there, but sometimes something unusual happens to save us from harm that leaves us scratching our heads. An incident happened to me once when I was driving a U-Haul truck late at night. I was feeling very sleepy and just as I dozed off, the radio turned on by itself with the volume turned up high, waking me up with a start. I have never been able to figure out how that happened.

Angels used to appear to prophets in human form. During the time of Prophet Muhammad, his companions once saw a stranger in clean white clothes talking to him. When the man left and they went after him, they found that he had vanished without a trace.[3] At other times, Gabriel would appear to the Prophet and talk with him, but others were not able to see him.[4] Sometimes angels would appear in human form in the Prophet's dreams.[5]

People can sometimes see angels in a dream state, and on rare occasions even interact with them in human form while awake. In that case, angels look and act human, which makes it difficult to tell whether they are angels or not.

In heaven, angels will be fully visible from the time of resurrection, as each person will be led to the judgment place by two angels. "The Trumpet will be sounded: 'This is the Day [you were] warned of.' Each person will arrive attended by an [angel] to drive him on and another to bear witness: 'You paid no attention to this [Day].'" (50:20-22)

On entering heaven, people will be greeted by angels. "They will enter perpetual Gardens, along with their righteous ancestors, spouses, and descendants; the angels will go in to them from every gate, 'Peace be with you, because you have remained steadfast. What an excellent reward is this home of yours!'" (13:23-24)

Later, when they're settled down in their new homes, people will have regular interaction with angels. An angel will arrive every week with an invitation for a meeting with God; there will be angels at the gathering and angels attending the markets from where people will receive gifts.

The angels in heaven will most likely be in human form, although some may appear in their original shape. "Praise be to God, Creator of the heavens and earth, who made angels messengers with two, three, four [pairs of] wings. He adds to creation as He will: God has power over everything." (35:1)

By saying that they could have different numbers of wings, the above verse suggests that not all angels are alike. The Prophet saw Gabriel in his original form on two occasions, and he appeared with six hundred wings.[6] It is likely that angels come in infinite shapes and sizes based on what task they have been designed to perform.

Ghilman

There will be a special class of eternally youthful, human-like beings in heaven who will act as servants, companions, and spouses for people in heaven. The males are called *ghilman*, while females are called *houri*. They will be very good-looking, well mannered, and beautifully dressed. When you're socializing with friends, ghilman will be serving you. "Devoted youths like hidden pearls wait on them." (52:24)

Ghilman have been mentioned in the Qur'an another time as serving drinks at a gathering. "Everlasting youths will attend them—if you could see them, you would think they were scattered pearls." (76:19) Out of the three times ghilman are mentioned in the Qur'an, twice they're described as being as beautiful as pearls, a term also used for houris.

Twice the Qur'an calls them *wildan mukhalladun*, which means "everlasting youths"[7] and once they're called *ghilman*, meaning "servants."[8]

Ghilman will look and act fully human, but they won't have free will, as far as we know, and they'll be created to be fully devoted to you and do whatever you ask them to.

Female houris are mentioned as wives for males who go to heaven. No similar suggestion has been made about ghilman being husbands for females, but it has been said that no one will be without a spouse in heaven. Therefore, it is said that a female who goes to heaven and doesn't have a human husband will be married to a ghilman especially created for her. And he will be the dream husband from her wildest fantasies. Make a list of whatever you wish for in a husband, and your husband in heaven will be far better than that.

Both males and females who go to heaven will get thousands of ghilman and houris as their personal servants looking after their mansions and property and serving them. A figure mentioned in one hadith for the minimum number of ghilman each person will get is eighty thousand.[9]

Houris

Apart from seeing God, houris are probably the reward that people, or at least men, look forward to more than anything else in heaven.

The word houri is derived from the Arabic *hur al-ayn*, which refers to eyes with very intense black irises and pure white sclera, or the white of the eye. Houris are beautiful human-like females with large, lovely eyes, who have been especially created for the inhabitants of heaven. Each person will get at least two houris as wives, while people in higher ranks will get more.

Houris have been mentioned in the Qur'an multiple times. "They will have pure spouses and there they will stay." (2:25) "With them will be spouses—modest of gaze and beautiful of eye—like protected eggs." (37:48-49) "They will have well-matched [wives] with modest gaze." (38:52) "We shall wed them to maidens with large, dark eyes." (44:54) "We pair them with beautiful-eyed maidens." (52:20) "There will be maidens restraining their glances, untouched beforehand by man or jinn." (55:56) "Like rubies and brilliant pearls." (55:58) "There are good-natured, beautiful maidens." (55:70) "Dark-eyed, sheltered in pavilions." (55:72) "and beautiful companions like hidden pearls: a reward for what they used to do." (56:22-24) "with incomparable companions We have specially created—virginal, loving, of matching age." (56:34-37) "nubile, well-matched companions." (78:33)

Houris are good-natured, young females with large, dark eyes and modest gaze with which they only look at their husbands and no one else. Some of them look like rubies and pearls. They have been especially created in heaven and live in mansions protected by angels, with no males being given access to them until the day they will meet their husbands from earth. Their virginity is not only physical but also emotional, as they will have had no past associations with anyone else to distract them from the love for their husbands. They know nothing but luxury, never having had to go through the hardship of this world. They laugh, sing, and are grateful to their husbands because their own creation and existence are on account of them.

Houris have been described as having perfect female forms and, as mentioned later for humans in heaven, they do not have any bodily excretions—no toilet functions, spitting, bleeding, etc. They do not have any childbearing anatomical functions and do not get pregnant.[10]

Like humans in heaven, houris will be perpetually young and free of any disease. They will have very sweet natures with no jealousy, hatred, malice, or resentment. Their language will be devoid of any coarse speech. Their love will be reserved exclusively for their husbands, and they will not even look at any other man.

They will have very delicate, thin, white skin and translucent bodies, and you'll be able to see right through them, like looking though a red ruby gemstone. Their faces will have almost mirror-like skin. They will be dressed in dozens of layers of semi-transparent clothes, and light will pass right through their clothes and bodies.[11]

Because they're created with a natural desire for a specific person, houris' lives revolve around the anticipation of meeting their husbands. Every man has at least two houris created and waiting for him. According to the Prophet, a houri is aware of the activities of her future husband in this world and considers herself to be his rightful wife, even while he is on earth. If he has an argument with his wife in this world, the houri mocks her and says something like, "Do, not annoy him; may God destroy you, for he is just a temporary guest with you and soon he will leave you and join us."[12]

According to one narration, when a man destined for heaven will be on his way to his mansion in heaven for the first time, a ghilman will run ahead and tell one of the houris waiting for her husband, "So-and-so has arrived," using the name by which he was called in this world. "You saw him!" she will cry, and he will answer, "I saw him indeed, and he's following me." Overcome by rapture, she will rush to the door to wait for him.[13] Then, when they first lay eyes on each other, they will just stare at each other for a very long time, unable to move. The man will not be able to believe how beautiful she is, and he himself will be outstandingly handsome as well. Every time he will turn away from her and then look back, she will appear even more beautiful than before.

One of the Prophet's wives asked him that if houris are so beautiful, then what about the women of this world. He told her that in heaven the women of this world will be even more beautiful than the houris, and that will be so because they've lived on this earth, worshipped God and suffered hardship, because of which their status will be higher in the eyes of God than that of the houris, and they will surpass the houris in beauty by a good margin.[14]

The Prophet said, "If a houri from paradise appeared to the people of the earth, she would fill the space between heaven and the earth with light and a pleasant scent and her head cover is better than the world and whatever is in it."[15]

Each man in heaven will be married to at least two houris, and their nature will be such that there will be no jealousy among them. In any case, the mansions in heaven will be so large that wives will not come across each other, even if they're living in the same house.

There is a description of one houri in heaven called Alina, which means "beautiful," who walks with seventy thousand servants walking to her left and another seventy thousand walking to her right as she is saying, "Where are those who enjoin good and forbid evil?"[16]

There is said to be one houri in heaven who is the most beautiful of them all. Her name is Laibah, which means "playful." She is so beautiful that if death were possible in heaven, looking at her would cause a person to die.[17] On the upper portion of her chest is written, "He who wants to possess one like me must obey my Lord, the exalted and glorious."[18]

There will be occasions when the houris will get together and sing, "We will live forever and we will never die. We live in blessings and will never grieve. We are pleased (with our husbands) and will never be displeased. Happy are they who are for us and we for them."[19]

Animals

We will discuss two categories of animals: the animals of this world and the animals of heaven. While there is some debate about whether animals from this world will go to heaven, for example cherished pets, the Qur'an and Hadith definitely confirm the presence of animals in heaven.

One of the verses of the Qur'an that hints at animals' being brought back to life on the Day of Resurrection says, "All the creatures that crawl on the earth and those that fly with their wings are communities like yourselves. We have missed nothing out of the Record—in the end they will be gathered to their Lord." (6:38) One interpretation of this verse is that on the Day of Resurrection, animals will be resurrected as well.

There is a hadith according to which animals that have harmed each other will be able to settle their scores against each other on the Day of Judgment. Some scholars say that after justice has been done, God will say to the animals, "be dust," and they will disintegrate and become dust.[20]

Some scholars have said that certain animals that have been mentioned in the Qur'an related to stories about prophets, will be in heaven, such as the ram that Abraham sacrificed instead of Ismael, the dog belonging to the Companions of the Cave, and some others.

A man asked the Prophet if there would be camels in heaven, and his reply was that in heaven, he would have whatever he wished. Therefore, the best answer to the question of whether your pet dog or cat will be in heaven is that God himself will routinely ask you if you wish for anything more, and therefore, if your pet is what you want, then God will be able to bring it back to life for you.

In Qur'anic verses related to heaven, the only type of animals that have been mentioned are birds, as sources of meat for food. Talking about people in heaven eating and drinking, the Qur'an says that they will have the choice of "The meat of any bird they like." (56:21)

Several types of animals have been mentioned in the Hadith. The Prophet mentioned birds that fly around heaven eating its fruits and drinking from its rivers. He also talked about beef and fish liver as items on the menu, suggesting that there would be cattle and fish. Camels were mentioned as something people would be able to have if they really wanted them.

At one time the Prophet said, "Sheep are among the animals of paradise."[21]

When someone asked the Prophet if there would be horses in heaven, he replied that there would be winged, flying horses made out of red rubies that would not have any bodily functions. My own interpretation of this is that they will be flying mechanical transportation devices, like aircraft, not actually horses. During the time of the Prophet, the sole purpose for keeping horses was for transport, and the questioner's intention may have been to find out if there would be something to travel on, and the Prophet answered in the affirmative and called it a winged horse.

Beyond that, I would suppose that if we wanted different kinds of animals, we will be able to get them. I would love to have pet lions, and I can imagine that I might be able to keep a whole pride of lions that will look and behave exactly like lions on earth, but they won't bite.

From the available information, it doesn't seem as though there will be jungles full of naturally occurring wild animals like we have on earth. Heaven will not have an environment like we have now, where all types of creatures have evolved. For example, I don't expect that the gardens in heaven will be full of worms and insects that make up the vast majority of living creatures on earth. I expect that only those animals will exist that are useful, like birds and cattle meant for eating, but the rest of the food chain will be missing, like bacteria, insects, reptiles, and the rest of the endless kinds of living things we have on earth.

Jinn and Extraterrestrials

Angels, ghilman, and houris are beings that dwell in heaven, and humans who go there will interact with them on a regular basis—daily in the case of ghilman and houris. There will also be other intelligent beings from this universe that will have arrived in heaven after going through a process of judgment, like humans. They will be there in their own part of heaven and will likely have little contact with humans, although I believe it will be possible for us to meet them if we want to. These will be the jinn and extraterrestrial beings from other planets.

Jinn are nonmaterial beings with free will that live on this earth but are invisible to us. They live and die as we do and will be resurrected on the Day of Judgment and will be judged and sent to heaven or hell. Since their physical form is very different from our own, their version of heaven is also likely to be different from the one we will inhabit. Since Satan and his helpers are jinn and they're convinced of their own superiority over humans, it means that they're quite satisfied with their nonmaterial forms; therefore, they're not likely to be resurrected in physical bodies like humans. So their dwelling place in heaven will need to be separate and customized for them, and there is likely to be little interaction between humans and jinn, unless they want to meet out of curiosity.

There is a hadith that mentions that heaven will be so large that people from hundreds of other worlds, many much larger than our own, will also be living there.[22] A verse in the Qur'an also suggests the existence of other inhabited worlds. "Among His signs is the creation of the heavens and earth and all the living creatures He has scattered throughout them: He has the power to gather them all together whenever He will." (42:29) Saying that living creatures are scattered throughout the universe implies the existence of many inhabited worlds.

Beings from other planets in this universe may be human-like, in which case their environment in heaven will be similar to ours, or some of them may have different forms, in which case they might get a different environment. Like jinn, I believe that they will dwell separately from humans, but it will probably be possible to meet them if we like.

It would be interesting to see if extraterrestrial beings look like humans or have all sorts of different forms. I am reminded of a movie, *Men in Black*, in which many extraterrestrials were together in a room and they came in a wide variety of shapes and sizes. It is possible that in heaven we might encounter all kinds of beings with radically different appearances.

6

Entering Heaven

In this chapter, we finally come to the part we've been waiting for—entering heaven. After judgment, once you've traveled across the As-Sirat Bridge, you will find yourself at the gates of heaven, ready to finally enter a place as big as the universe, where you'll be spending the next few billion years of your life, or eternity.

Trying to visualize what the gates of heaven will be like, I would say that since heaven will be a universe, and a universe consists of planetary bodies, this place will also be a planet, this time located in close proximity to, or on the edge of, the galaxies making up heaven.

If indeed this is a planet, and heaven will consist of millions of them, then what we call the "gates of heaven" cannot be like typical gates on earth, where on one side of the gate you're outside some place, and once you enter the gate, you're inside, implying that part of the planet is heaven and part of it is not.

If you imagine heaven to be a large, walled city, then you may think of a gate of heaven being like an ordinary gate with security guards checking your credentials and allowing you to enter. If you imagine heaven to be the size of a whole country, like America, then you may imagine a gate of heaven to be like a border crossing with immigration officials examining your passport and letting you in.

The heaven we're talking about here is larger than this whole universe. Therefore, what we call a gate, I imagine will be more like a transport hub from where you will fly to another planet that will be your real home.

Because this planet will be on the edge of heaven, I believe that, while this planet will not be exactly like heaven, it will be a much more pleasant place than the planet where resurrection and judgment will have recently taken place. We will arrive here in the same bodies that we will be resurrected in, so the environment of this place will need to be suitable for human bodies similar to the ones we have on earth, but since our earthly bodies will then be transformed into superior bodies that we will have in heaven, the environment will need to be suitable for those new bodies as well. While we are on this planet, it cannot be said that we have entered heaven yet. Even though this planet will be nice, the environment, weather, buildings, and everything else in heaven will be far better.

Unlike the planet of resurrection, which in most accounts is said to have a mostly barren landscape, I believe this place will be fully built-up with lots of physical structures. As soon as we arrive there by traveling across the As-Sirat Bridge, we are likely to find ourselves among buildings and paved, open public spaces.

There are several functions that this planet will fulfill. One is that, being much closer to heaven compared to the planet of resurrection, it will allow easy access to heaven. People will have traveled a vast distance by crossing the As-Sirat Bridge to arrive there. Distance from here to people's final destinations will be much shorter, and there will be some form of vehicular transportation available for traveling there.

This planet will house sorting facilities where people will show their records of judgment to angels who will then direct them to their correct destinations in heaven. Billions of people will be traveling to different locations, so it's not hard to imagine that there will be lots of activity going on, and there will be large numbers of angels supervising activities.

Before entering the gates, people will have their bodies and souls transformed in preparation for a life in heaven, and that will happen on this planet. The new body and clothes each person will get will depend on what grade of heaven they've been assigned to, and angels on this planet will need to make sure that the crowds are properly organized and everyone gets to their final destination without a hitch.

Since people will be arriving at the gates with bodies and behavior similar to those we have now, people may still be subject to getting tired, irritable, or angry, and their behavior patterns could be similar to how crowds behave on earth, potentially creating situations that may get out of control. Expect the angels to be polite but firm in the way they treat people at this point. Once their bodies and psyche have been changed in preparation for entering heaven, people's behavior will be entirely different, and the angels' demeanor will also become a lot more courteous.

I imagine that the actual gates of heaven will be massive spaceport facilities like in science-fiction movies. Once you enter the gate, you will proceed to a platform where a spaceship will fly you to your home in heaven. Since heaven has eight gates, this planet might have eight of these spaceport terminals with a paved, open space, like a public square, in between, where millions of people will be gathering.

The gates of heaven have been described as each being hundreds of miles wide. Therefore, since distances will be vast and people will still have frail bodies, there are also likely to be transport facilities, such as trains, to take people to their correct gates.

In addition, there will be lakes where people will go to have drinks, and there will be facilities on this planet where people will swim in pools to have their bodies transformed and will get new clothes.

When you arrive here, you will find yourself in a vast open space where people will be congregating, arriving in quick succession after having received judgment, and crossing the As-Sirat Bridge. At this point, people will still have the ordinary bodies in which they were resurrected.

The first thing they'll do when they arrive here, will be to have a drink. Most people will proceed to get a drink, but some people will have to pass yet another hurdle.

Settling Scores

While most people will be going for a drink, there will be a class of people who will be detained for a while. These will be the ones who have unsettled quarrels with each other that they never resolved or forgave on earth.

At this point in time, they will be required to settle their differences before proceeding any further.[1]

During the judgment process, God would have forgiven the sins of those granted entry into heaven, but if they have pending issues with each other, they will be required to settle them at this point. They will be able to talk it over and forgive each other or maybe retaliate physically to get even; whichever way they settle matters between themselves, they would need to do so before rejoining the crowds and moving forward towards the gates of heaven.

The idea behind this is that while God forgives sins committed against him, he does not forgive a sin committed against another person. Only that person can forgive it. If you committed an injustice against someone and both of you happen to be going to heaven, you will meet that person here and will have to make amends.

Cistern of Kauthar

After crossing the As-Sirat Bridge, people will proceed towards an area where they will be given drinks from the rivers of heaven. All the prophets will have cisterns, or founts, of their own of various sizes, filled with water from heaven, and they'll be waiting to receive their followers to give them drinks. Some prophets will have millions of followers and their cisterns will be very large—the size of lakes, or seas. Some prophets will have only one or two followers, and some will have none.[2] There were innumerable prophets sent to the world, and while some were successful and gained many adherents, there were others who were able to convince only a few people, and there were some with no followers at all. The total number of prophets is said to have been in the region of one hundred and twenty-five thousand, with Prophet Muhammad being the very last one, and there will be none after him.

The cistern of Prophet Muhammad, called the Cistern of Kauthar,[3] will be a square-shaped lake, with each side being hundreds of miles wide.[4] It will be fed with water from the River of Kauthar (River of Abundance) that flows in heaven. There will be two pipes bringing in the water from heaven, one of which will be made of gold and the other one of silver,[5] suggesting that one pipe will be bringing water from the upper level of heaven and the other one from the lower level. There will be countless cups placed by the banks of the lake, and its water will be whiter than milk and sweeter than honey. You'll be able to pick up a cup, fill it from the lake, and have a drink, and when you drink that water, you'll never be thirsty again.

Some scholars have suggested that the Cistern of Kauthar will be located before the As-Sirat Bridge, while others insist that you will find it after crossing the bridge. My own inclination is towards accepting the latter point of view because, after crossing the As-Sirat Bridge, you would have arrived at the planet where the gates of heaven will be located, which will be at the edge of heaven, and it's easier to imagine water from heaven flowing to this nearby location rather than to the planet of resurrection that will be located a long distance away, beyond hell. Either way, after the pronouncement of judgment, but before entering the gates of heaven, you will get a drink from Prophet Muhammad's Cistern of Kauthar, or from one belonging to another prophet. The Prophet told his followers that they would find him in one of three locations—by the scales at the time of judgment, by the As-Sirat Bridge, or at the Cistern of Kauthar.[6] He will be advancing along the same route that everyone else will follow, except that he'll be ahead of others.

If you're a follower of another prophet, such as Moses or Jesus, they will also be there next to their own cisterns, and you'll be able to find them and receive a drink. Don't count on any prophet personally greeting you and giving you a drink, since there will be too many people there. There will be angels making sure that only followers of a particular prophet drink at their cistern and others will be turned away.

The Prophet said that some people would try to approach his cistern but will be prevented from doing so because they will not have followed his teachings properly and will therefore not be considered part of his community.[7] Some take this as an indication that those people will be going to hell and therefore that is the main reason why it is thought that the Cistern of Kauthar will be located before the As-Sirat Bridge; because everyone who would have reached this point will be bound for heaven. But my own interpretation is that even though those people who will have been turned away from the Cistern of Kauthar may have been excommunicated from the community of Prophet Muhammad, it doesn't necessarily mean that they will be going to hell. It is possible that they might be going to heaven without being considered part of the Prophet's community, maybe because God will have forgiven their sins.

It may be asked why it will be so important which prophet you followed and why people will be divided into groups based on which prophet they believed in. I don't think that once you enter heaven, it would matter much, since there's no hadith about the Prophet saying that inhabitants of heaven will get different treatment based on which religion they have followed. If you're entering heaven, it will mean that you're a member of the fellowship of believers. Once in heaven, people will mix together and be part of the same community. But the Prophet did mention that there will be some brotherly competition between prophets to see whose followers enter heaven in the largest numbers.[8] Prophet Muhammad was shown a vision about the Day of Judgment in which he saw his own followers in such vast numbers that they filled up the whole horizon,[9] and he saw this vision at a time when he had hardly a few dozen supporters.

After having a drink, you will move on towards the gates of heaven.

The Gates of Heaven

Heaven will have eight gates. They cannot be like the gates that we might see outside a royal palace, since hundreds of millions of people will be entering through them. They've been described as hundreds of miles wide, but even then feeling narrow because of the vast numbers of people entering through them.[10]

Each gate is named after good qualities that earned people entry into heaven. There will be the Gate of Charity, Gate of Prayers, Gate of Fasting, Gate of Struggle (in God's path), Gate of Faith, Gate of Repentance, Gate of Satisfaction (with God), Gate of Forgiveness (for those who forgive others). The first four names come from a hadith of the Prophet,[11] while the rest have been derived from other sources. According to the Prophet, people will enter through the gate that corresponds to their best quality, e.g., if they fasted a lot or were very charitable, while some people of particularly good standing will be allowed to pass through whichever gate they choose. Assuming that you're allowed to enter from any gate you want, angels will approach you inviting you to come though their gate. It's like they'll be competing against each other to see which gate attracts the most people.

The Prophet said, "If anyone testifies that none has the right to be worshipped but God alone who has no partners, and that Muhammad is his slave and his apostle, and that Jesus is God's slave and his apostle and his word which he bestowed on Mary and a spirit created by him, and that heaven is true, and hell is true, God will admit him into paradise with the deeds which he had done even if those deeds were few. Such a person can enter paradise through any of its eight gates he likes."[12]

It's not been made clear in religious texts what the gates of heaven will look like and what exactly we'll find once we enter. Would there be a walled city with gates through which we will enter? Would the climate inside the gates be different from what it is outside?

I have used a mixture of logic and imagination to try to figure out what it will be like to enter the gates of heaven. I have pondered the issue, and here is my conclusion. As I've mentioned before, we will be on a planet on the edge of heaven, but this place will not have all the characteristics of heaven. When we arrive here in our earth-like bodies, we will not find buildings and streets made of gold and silver, like heaven is supposed to have. This planet will be a place of transition between the planet of resurrection and heaven.

The eight gates of heaven will be vast structures hundreds of miles in width that will be like enormous airport terminals from where people will be transported to the real heaven. When it is said that you will enter the gates of heaven, you will actually be entering these terminal buildings and once inside, you will find that they are built and decorated to the standards of heaven, meaning the inside of the terminals will be of gold, silver, and gemstones.

To get an idea of what I'm talking about, imagine that you're from a wealthy state visiting the capital city of a country that is poor and underdeveloped that has hot and unpleasant weather. It does, however, have a brand-new airport built by some advanced nation as a gift. When you're due to catch a flight back to your own country, you drive through the chaotic streets of the city, and when you reach the airport and enter the terminal building, you find yourself in beautiful surroundings similar to an airport in your own country. Outside the airport, it is hot, humid, and disorderly, but once you're inside the terminal building, you find yourself in an air-conditioned, neat, and clean environment. As soon as you walk through the doors, it feels like you've already arrived back in your home country.

Similarly, these transport terminals will be outposts of heaven located on a planet that will not itself be part of heaven. Think of how cities are sometimes called gateways to a country; for example, Hong Kong is called the gateway to China. Melbourne Airport in Australia aspires to be a gateway to China as well. There's a huge arch-like structure in St. Louis, Missouri, called the Gateway Arch, and it's referred to as the Gateway to the West.

A gate is an entry point to some place. One characteristic of a gate is that one side usually faces the exterior of a location. So the exterior of the gates of heaven would have to be located in a place that is not heaven. If this whole planet were a part of heaven, then you would already be in heaven while you were still outside the gates. The only thing that makes logical sense is to assume that the whole planet will be a gateway to heaven and the actual gates will be transportation hubs.

And that's how I see it—that the gates of heaven are transportation hubs, and as soon as you enter one of the terminal buildings, you'll feel like you've entered heaven, although you'll still need to travel some distance on a spacecraft to reach your new home. Once you will arrive at your home planet, the climate will be totally different from what it will be like on this planet, and the buildings and streets and everything else will be of a quality far beyond what they will be like here. With that in mind, let's carry on.

Outside the gates of heaven, before entering, everyone will have their bodies and souls transformed in preparation for a new life. Before reaching the gates, people will come to a place where there will be two streams. Drinking from the first one will change their souls, and bathing in the second one will transform their bodies.[13]

Let's try to put things in the order that they will happen. After drinking from the cisterns of the prophets, people will move towards the gates of heaven. Each of these gates will be like an enormous terminal building, and we could imagine these buildings to be circular in shape. The way it might work is that people will approach from all sides and pass through various stages to get to the main structure of each gate, which is in the center. As they get nearer, they will first encounter an outer ring of buildings, where people will get a soul-transforming drink. Having passed through that, they will approach another ring of buildings with swimming pools, where their bodies will be transformed. Then, they will be dressed in new clothes, and next they will proceed to an area with open public spaces, where they will collect in groups. This space will be an inner loop around the main

Entering Heaven 127

building. Then, finally, they will pass though the doors and enter into the terminal buildings.

First, they will pass through the ring of buildings providing the soul-transforming drink. As soon as they drink the water, all negativity will leave their souls, and they will find themselves feeling relaxed and in a happy mood.

Then they will pass through and enter the next set of buildings with pools from the River of Life and take a dip in the water. Once people's bodies will have been transformed, they will increase in size from an average height of five-and-a-half feet to ninety feet.[14] We're assuming that when people will be resurrected, not only will they have bodies biologically similar to the ones we have now, but their bodies will be the same size as their existing ones. But since the Prophet said that our height in heaven will be ninety feet, this means that swimming in the River of Life will increase our size tremendously.

After getting new bodies, people will be dressed in new clothes, and they will exit from the other end of the River of Life facility to collect in another public space, where their prophets will accompany them. There, they will wait for a while until the doors open, and then they will enter the terminal building. Once they will enter, the environment inside will be controlled to match the climate in heaven, kind of like entering an air-conditioned airport terminal located in a hot desert. The inside of the terminal will be designed and built to the standards of heaven, and that will be the moment when it can be said that a person has passed the gates and entered heaven.

Our Altered Psyche

In this world, the human soul is capable of a wide range of positive and negative emotions. The negative side of our behavior may be related to our bodies or to our souls. If we're hungry, we feel irritable, whereas if we take certain medicines, they may have a calming influence on us. That tells us that the physical makeup of our bodies has an effect on our thoughts and feelings; therefore, if we're going to get perfect bodies in heaven, it can be expected that all negativity will be removed from us.

The position scientists would take is that if we had perfect bodies, our behavior would also be perfect, because they consider the physical body to be all there is, and that all human behavior is governed by the flow of chemical or electrical signals in our bodies. In contrast, if we believe that humans have souls, then we also need to attribute some of our feelings and emotions to our souls.

The reality is that our feelings are more than just a consequence of bodily functions. There are many negative thoughts and feelings that seem to spring from within our souls that cannot simply be explained by the flow of hormones in our blood—feelings such as jealousy, envy, greed, pride, hate, etc. Even wealthy people in perfect physical condition suffer from negative thinking. It's not just our bodies that incline us towards evil; our souls also have negative tendencies.

It is possible that we were given these emotions because, in controlled doses, they might make us more competitive in this world by motivating us to work harder to be successful, and therefore might even be beneficial. For example, if people were not greedy for material possessions, human societies may not have progressed economically. But when they're not controlled, these emotions can become destructive and, in my opinion, are responsible for many of the problems we have in the world today.

Heaven has no place for negative feelings, whether they arise from the body or from the soul. Adam and Eve were expelled from heaven when they ate the forbidden fruit and switched on the negative characteristics of their psyche. Before that, they were incapable of negative thought.

Some people develop deep resentments about some real or perceived wrongs done to them, and this consumes them to the point where they can no longer enjoy life, no matter how comfortable a life they're living. If such emotions are allowed to exist in heaven, they can easily ruin the whole experience. Frankly, we would not want to go to heaven to live for millions of years thinking the same negative thoughts that haunt us here on earth. In that case, living for eternity could become intolerable.

We will be cleansed of all unwanted thought processes while we're still outside the gates of heaven when we will drink from one of the two streams. It will cause all negativity to be eliminated from us, and we will no longer have any bad thoughts. The Qur'an says, "We shall have removed all ill feeling from their hearts." (7:43) It also says, "But the righteous will be in Gardens with springs—"Enter them in peace and safety!"—and We shall remove any bitterness from their hearts: [they will be like] brothers, sitting on couches, face to face. No weariness will ever touch them there, nor will they ever be expelled." (15:45-48)

Another thing that's been mentioned is that people's thinking in heaven will become very much alike, and they will act in unison on many matters, such as answering God as one person in reply to his questions. This similarity in thinking will remove the potential of disagreements among them and maintain harmony.

Our memories will still be there, even bad ones; it's just that they will no longer trouble us. The reason for being allowed to continue to remember bad things that

Entering Heaven 131

happened to us is that memories make us who we are. If you lose your memories, you will no longer be the same person. In heaven, you will be the same person, and you will have perfect recollection of everything that happened to you on earth, and you will remember everyone you met and interacted with. The Qur'an describes people in heaven discussing their lives on earth, including the hardships they suffered.

An example of preserved memories among the people in heaven is the following verse in the Qur'an: "They will turn to one another with questions: one will say, 'I had a close companion on earth who used to ask me, "Do you really believe that after we die and become dust and bone, we shall be brought back for judgment?"' Then he will say, 'Shall we look for him?' He will look down and see him in the midst of the Fire, and say to him, 'By God, you almost brought me to ruin! Had it not been for the grace of my Lord, I too would have been taken to Hell.'" (37:50-57)

Talking about retaining memories, you'll even remember reading this book. Allow me to plant a thought in your mind for the time when you're in heaven and remember reading this. Compare what was written in this book with what you actually see in heaven, and then find me, if I'm there, and let me know. Ask one of the angels, and he'll tell you how to locate me. That will give me a good idea of whether this book helped anyone get into heaven.

According to some accounts, when people drink at the Cistern of Kauthar, that is when their psyche will be changed. If that is so, then the stream we're talking about is actually the Cistern of Kauthar. The next stream will be the River of Life that will alter our bodies.

Our Bodies

When we dip into the second stream outside the gates of heaven, our bodies will be totally transformed into ones that are different from the bodies we have now. Up to this point in our journey, we will have had earth-like bodies, so when we're given new bodies, that may be the moment when the realization will fully dawn upon people that heaven will be much more than what they had imagined it to be. Not everyone will know what to expect, so for a lot of people, everything going on will be a strange experience. After the transformation, we will be changing into the form that Adam and Eve had while they were still in heaven the first time.[15]

This stream is the one that is called the River of Life in many accounts. Swimming in it transforms people's bodies into eternal ones that never die.

The way it may work is that we will enter an enormous room with a very large swimming pool. We will be asked to get into the water and swim across. We will still be the same size we are now, so the pool will appear to be very large, but as we get into the water, our bodies will increase in size and be transformed, and as we begin to emerge from the water on the other end of the pool, the surroundings may not seem so huge anymore. What if you don't know how to swim? As soon as you get into the water, your body will change very quickly, and you'll find that you can swim like an expert. Many new skills will be preprogrammed into our brains in our new bodies, and swimming will probably be one of them.

Once inside the water, everyone will become exceedingly beautiful, both men and women, with the inhabitants of the higher levels of heaven being the most beautiful. The least person will be as good as, if not better than, the most beautiful person who has ever lived on earth. Their appearance has been compared to the prophet Joseph, who was renowned for his physical beauty.[16]

The Prophet told us that our height would be sixty cubits, which equates to ninety feet.[17] That would be so if a person from heaven were to come down to earth, but since we will be in a different environment, the dimensions there will be different. Since everything else will be correspondingly bigger, it will not feel odd in any way. It will not be as though trees or houses will suddenly start feeling tiny because we've become so large.

The new bodies will have no bodily excretions except sweat—no toilet functions, spitting, sneezing, bleeding, runny noses, etc.[18] We will still eat and drink, but excess matter will be eliminated in the form of sweet-smelling sweat and burps.[19]

My own conjecture is that the special food of heaven, whether it is solid or liquid, once swallowed, will melt into liquid form and diffuse throughout the body. We will probably not have the same type of internal organs as we do now, and food will be immediately digested and dissipated through the skin into the air as evaporated sweat at the same rate as it is eaten. We have been told that we will be able to eat continuously, as long as we like, without ever feeling full. This will overcome the limitation imposed on us when our stomachs become full before our desire for a tasty meal is fully satisfied. Since food in heaven will be a lot tastier than food on earth, and available in very large quantities and variety, we will want to eat a lot more.

Both men and women will have no body hair, except on the head. Men will be free of facial hair, and they will not have beards, nor will they need to shave.[20] There will be no one, not even prophets, with flowing white beards, as depicted in paintings.

Every person will be the same age, thirty years old (some accounts say thirty-three), no matter what age they were at the time of death, whether still-born babies or very old.[21] This age is relative to this world; in heaven, age has no meaning, since people will have been recreated that way and will be living for a long time, but the idea is that if you tried to guess the age of someone in heaven, they will look like a person who in this world is around thirty years old, that is, people won't look like teenagers or middle-aged people. This will apply to both men and women.

There will be no further aging in heaven, and people will stay exactly the same forever. There will be no disease, and everyone will stay healthy and fit.[22] On entering heaven, we will hear an announcement: "You will live forever and you will be healthy forever."[23]

It is not stated whether people will in any way be susceptible to injury if they fall, or whether they will feel pain from getting hit by something. The general idea is that heaven will be a technologically advanced environment where all dangers will have been totally eliminated, and no one will be likely to get injured. That's one of the things we're always trying to achieve on earth, with safety standards of today being much better than they were a hundred years ago, and we're continuously trying to improve things in an attempt to achieve a zero-injury environment. Heaven will be a zero-injury environment.

The pain our bodies feel when we suffer an injury or disease serves a beneficial role here on earth because it alerts us to something being wrong and requiring attention. If we didn't feel any pain when we place our hand on a hot surface, then we would not remove it quickly enough to avoid damaging our skin. Therefore, pain helps in protecting us from an even more serious injury. But in heaven, since there will be no threat of injury or disease, the need for pain will be obsolete, and we will thankfully be free of all pain.

The Prophet told us that people will have black hair and large eyes that will look like they've had kohl, which is like mascara, applied to them.[24] If someone wants blonde, brunette, red, or even purple hair, then I'm sure those options will be available. In fact, people will be able to change their appearance whenever they like.

Skin will be white.[25] There will be no racial or ethnic divisions in heaven. There will be no major physical differences between people, as there are on earth, where some people are tall, some short, some thin, some fat, etc. In fact, it has been said that everyone will look alike, although they'll be recognizable as individuals.

People will have enhanced sexual functions[26]—again, with the negative side effects eliminated; therefore, there will be no bodily fluids, no risk of disease, and no pregnancies.[27]

Everyone will be exceedingly strong, and there will be no fatigue or feelings of hunger or thirst.[28] People will eat for pleasure, not because they have to.

There will be no sleep in heaven.[29] Since there will be no fatigue, sleeping will not be necessary. There will be no darkness, only perpetual daylight. If someone would like some darkness, they'll be able to draw the curtains in their house.

Other than the above differences, everything else will be the same as now in terms of what we will look like and the functions of our various body parts. We will have eyes to see, ears to hear, noses to smell, fingers to touch, etc., but all our senses will likely be heightened. We will be able to see farther, perceive more colors, hear better, have a finer sense of touch, and so on.

Although it's not been specifically mentioned in any religious text, I would expect that we will be more intelligent than we are now. Our souls are capable of a high level of intelligence, but our physical bodies filter out much of our intelligence because of the more limited capabilities of our brains. We've been told that all souls are made the same way, which means that differences in our IQs are the result of the capacity of our physical brains, not our souls. If we will get improved bodies, then there should be no reason why all of us cannot have an IQ similar to the most intelligent people, somewhere in the region of 200.

Even though people will have been so thoroughly transformed, they will still be recognizable as the same person they were on earth. When you run into people you knew in this world, you'll be able to recognize them and they will recognize you.

On the Day of Resurrection, we will start out with bodies similar to the ones we have on earth, made with our DNA records, but then they will be transformed into perfect, everlasting bodies before we enter heaven. It is open to speculation whether these new bodies will be based on a biology similar to the one on earth with self-replicating cells that require constant nourishment, or whether they'll be based on a totally different biology. Doctors going to heaven will probably be curious to figure out how the new bodies work, and they may even have to take some extra medical courses. For doctors, there will be no relief from the need to study continuously, even in heaven, although they won't find any patients needing their services.

We will eat and drink. Some people say that food will not be required and will be consumed only for pleasure, but I think that the food we will eat will supply nutrients to our new bodies, and the reason it is said that there will be no hunger or thirst in heaven is because food and drink will always be available, not because bodies will be independent of nutritional requirements.

What will make these bodies everlasting will be their ability to constantly stay in an optimal condition by being fed with perfectly healthy food and drinks that will be prepared by expert ghilman chefs, and the lack of any toxic substances that can cause disease. Our bodies on earth are preprogrammed to age and wither away, no matter how well we take care of them, but with the new biology of heaven, there will be no aging process.

It has also been mentioned that we will be able to swim underwater for as long as we like without having to come up to breathe.[30]

Let's consider what may happen when you come out of the water after being transformed. You'll probably start by looking at your hands and turn them over to see what they look like, and you will see that they're beautiful. Then, you will look at your legs and chest, and try to look around to see if you can find a mirror. If it's an indoor setting, which I believe it will be, I wouldn't be surprised if there were huge mirrors available for you to look at yourself as you step out of the swimming pool. What you'll see is a stunningly beautiful body and face. You will still be able to recognize yourself, but your features will be a vast improvement over your former self.

Not everyone knows what to expect in heaven, so everything that would be happening, including getting new bodies, will all be unexpected events for them. Therefore, they can be expected to be flabbergasted when they see themselves in their new bodies.

Clothes

Once you've come out of the pool with a new, perfect body, there will be angels waiting with beautiful new clothes for you to wear. They will dress you like a king or queen.

Clothes worn by both men and women will be very fancy, and people of both sexes will wear jewelry made out of precious metals and gemstones. These clothes will always stay in perfect shape and never get creased, dirty, or wear out.[31] Clothes will be perfumed, and each layer of clothes you wear will have a different scent.

Your garments will be made of fine green silk and heavy brocade with gold embroidery, and you will be wearing bracelets of gold or silver studded with pearls and emeralds. "There they will be adorned with bracelets of gold. There they will wear green garments of fine silk and brocade." (18:31) "They will wear garments of green silk and brocade; they will be adorned with silver bracelets; their Lord will give them a pure drink." (76:21) On your head, you will wear a crown inlaid with precious jewels.[32]

Although the Qur'an mentions clothes of green silk, there is likely to be considerable variety of colors and designs. It has been said that your mansion will have rooms of different colors, and when you enter a room, the color of your clothes will automatically change to match the color scheme of the room.

According to the Prophet, clothes will not be woven, as they are on earth, but will grow on trees and come out of their fruits.[33] I understand this to mean that those trees will actually be like automatic machines that will manufacture and dispense clothes based on any design you choose. I believe that heaven will be a technologically advanced environment with high levels of automation.

If you want new clothes, you will find them on display at the market, or shopping mall, that you will visit at least once a week. You will be free to acquire as many as you want. Even though your old clothes will never wear out, you will still have an unlimited supply of new ones. Since your mansion will be very large, you may have a whole section of it devoted to storing your clothes. There will be no poor people to give away your used clothes to, but it is possible that you may be able to exchange clothes with others.

Some women's clothes have been described as being made of such fine material that wearing even dozens of layers would not make a person appear bulky. The clothes that houris will wear will be so fine and transparent that you'll be able to see right through them, even if they're wearing many layers.

Collecting Outside the Gates

After they've had their bodies and souls transformed, people will congregate in another vast open space just outside the eight gates or terminals. Everyone will be arranged in rows behind their prophets and will await permission to move forward. Before entering heaven, everyone will be arranged in a specific order. People will be divided into groups consisting of followers of various prophets, and within these groups, the best among them will be in the front. Once all the followers of one prophet will have entered, those of the next prophet will follow.

The Prophet said that in his vision of the gates of heaven, he saw poor people entering ahead of rich people. That is because they will have to give a lighter account of their possessions on earth. There will be more men than women.[34]

If you recall, everyone will have joined their respective prophets earlier, with the people of Prophet Muhammad meeting him at the Cistern of Kauthar, and others joining their own prophets at other locations. The Prophet said that people will be arranged in one hundred and twenty rows waiting to enter heaven, and up to eighty of the rows will be made up of his followers.[35]

People will finally be entering heaven after having gone through so many steps. Let's recall how we got here.

First, we were resurrected with bodies similar to our earthly ones on a planet that was geographically similar to earth. Then, we had to face God and go through the process of judgment. After judgment, we crossed the As-Sirat Bridge, which was like a wormhole from theoretical physics, and arrived on this planet that serves as the gateway to heaven and is located on the edge of heaven. When we arrived here, we were still in our earth-like bodies and capable of both good and bad feelings, such as fatigue, excitement, and fear. Then, we were transformed after drinking and bathing in the two streams and finally dressed up in clothes from heaven.

Family members will find each other before entering heaven and will be together now. There are many grades in heaven, and if it had happened that two family members were assigned to different grades at the time of judgment, it would have resulted in their being separated. To resolve this issue, a family member deserving a lower grade in heaven will be upgraded to a higher grade to be with their loved ones. No one will be downgraded. If your family member or spouse is destined for a higher grade in heaven, you have a good chance of getting upgraded to their level. Therefore, if family members help each other progress to a higher rank, they're helping themselves too.

Entering the Gates

Once our bodies and minds have been transformed and we're all dressed up in fancy new clothes, we will be ready to enter heaven.

The angel in charge of heaven is named Ridwan, and he is the commander of all the angels assigned to heaven, including those posted at the gates. Prophet Muhammad said that he would knock on one of the doors of heaven and Ridwan would open it and ask him who he is. He will reply, "Muhammad." Ridwan will say, "I have been commanded not to open heaven for anyone before you."[36] Then, he will welcome him and let him in, and the Prophet and his followers will enter heaven and then everyone else will follow.

Heaven is a hierarchical place, and everyone will receive honor and rewards according to their deeds on earth without arousing any resentment or jealousy, because negative feelings will have been banished forever.

The Prophet said, "The first group that will enter paradise will be like the moon on the night of the full moon. The second will be like the brightest star shining in the sky."[37] Everyone will now be ninety feet tall, have beautiful bodies and be dressed fabulously. If we could see now what people entering heaven will look like, we would probably be awestruck.

According to the Qur'an, angels will greet everyone as they enter. "They will enter perpetual Gardens, along with their righteous ancestors, spouses, and descendants; the angels will go in to them from every gate, 'Peace be with you, because you have remained steadfast. What an excellent reward is this home of yours!'" (13:23-24)

Angels will be congratulating everyone as they enter. The Qur'an states that, "Those who were mindful of their Lord will be led in throngs to the Garden. When they arrive, they will find its gates wide open, and its keepers will say to them, 'Peace be upon you. You have been good. Come in: you are here to stay,' and they will say, 'Praise be to God who has kept His promise to us and given us this land as our own. Now we may live wherever we please in the Garden.'" (39:73-74)

People will be entering through the gates of heaven in large crowds, maybe millions at a time, so you can imagine that the terminal buildings will be enormous, and the width of each gate has been described as being hundreds of miles wide. Think of it as entering the gates of Disneyland, but multiply everything by a few million, including the numbers of people entering and the size of the park itself.

Imagine being surrounded with your near and dear ones who have also made it into heaven. These will be your parents, grandparents, children, and grandchildren. But your grandparents may have their own grandparents with them and your grandchildren may have their own grandchildren. Family groups may get pretty large, but everyone will be of similar age and look just as beautiful. If you are a woman, you and your mother will look like twin sisters and your grandmother and great grandmother will also be the same age and just as pretty.

Another thing to keep in mind is that you will be the same person as you are now. You are what you are because of your memories, and you'll remember everything from your past life. Therefore, I believe that everyone will be in a state of bewilderment and excitement at the whole situation. Since all negativity will have been removed from your soul and heaven will be beautiful beyond imagination, it will mean that as soon as you enter it, you will be in a state of ecstasy and bliss, feelings that will remain for eternity.

Transportation to Heaven

Imagine that you're now in a spaceport terminal capable of handling millions of passengers simultaneously that resembles an airport but is vastly larger, more technologically advanced and beautiful than any airport you've ever seen. You will now be in a state of permanent happiness because of your altered psyche, have a gorgeous body, and be dressed like a king or queen. The spaceport facilities will need to be good enough to match your new condition, and that's why the terminal you'll be in will be far superior to anything you've ever seen before. The walls will be made of gold and silver and will be studded with precious stones.

Angels will be manning the terminal and directing people to their transfer stations. You will have your judgment record in your hand, which will have details about your final destination, and based on that, angels will tell you where you'll need to go. Or maybe they'll just recognize your face and know who you are; if we can have facial recognition technology on earth, it should be available in heaven also. There will be great throngs of people rushing in various directions, and you and your family will be trying to find your way around the crowd. What will make the sight truly amazing to behold will be that everyone will be beautiful beyond imagination and will be dressed like royalty. And, obviously, there will be no luggage, as everything you will ever need will be present in your new home.

Finally, you'll arrive at the correct spaceport, and your transport vehicle will be ready and waiting.

At the time of the Prophet, transportation consisted of ships for traveling on water and animals for traveling on land. Camels were used for everyday transportation and also for milk and meat, while horses were used for riding to war. Camels, therefore, served several purposes, while horses were only meant for riding. A companion of the Prophet asked him if there would be horses in heaven, and he replied that there would be winged horses made of red rubies that would not have any bodily functions and would fly you anywhere you want. In another hadith, the Prophet told his companions that on the Day of Judgment, people bound for heaven would be flown to their homes on winged horses made from red rubies.[38]

In various hadith narrations, the flying devices are described as being horses made out of red rubies, red pearls, red emeralds, or they're said to be white camels that look like pearls. In every instance, it is said that they will fly people to various locations in heaven.

My interpretation of these horses is that they will actually be flying machines with wings. They'll be made from, or decorated with, rubies or emeralds, just like everything else in heaven will be made from precious materials. The picture this creates in my mind is of beautiful, winged aircraft with some advanced form of propulsion that will fly between different locations in heaven, even between different planets. They will probably be available in various shapes and sizes for different uses. Some could be small, one-person craft, like a flying jet-ski on which you would ride while sitting externally, and these may look the most like some animal. Some could be larger, big enough to accommodate several people, and have an enclosed cabin. The ones for interplanetary travel could be bigger still and have seating for many, like a jetliner. It is likely that each person will have a whole fleet of these spacecraft of various sizes. Your aircraft will be your own, not shared, because there's such abundance in heaven that sharing will not be required.

There is another saying of the Prophet, not related to heaven, in which he mentioned that when the Antichrist will arrive on earth, he will fly over the clouds in a white donkey one hundred feet long.[39] The modern interpretation of this is that he was referring to modern-day aircraft. That is another reason why I believe that the winged horses in heaven will also be aircraft, or spacecraft. I doubt that the people of 1,400 years ago would have been able to understand the concept of aircraft or spaceships, and calling them horses, camels, or donkeys would have been the only way to explain such objects to them.

When you arrive at the correct gate, you and your family will enter your private spacecraft, the doors will close, and it will fly you to another planet, which will actually be part of heaven. Your first stop will be to attend a banquet. You will fly into a terminal on another planet and when you step out, you will finally be in heaven.

The Welcome Banquet

According to Prophet Muhammad, there will be a welcome banquet for people on entering heaven. It is likely to be held immediately on entering and before everyone will go to their mansions for the first time. The Prophet even told us what will be on the menu.

It is possible, however, that the welcome banquet will take place after everyone has gone to their mansions first, and then they will go to the welcome ceremony. It is also not clear if the banquet will be held in one place or in many different locations on various levels of heaven. It is possible that each grade of heaven may arrange its own welcoming banquet, and there might be a hundred or more banquets being held on different planets.

As you leave the terminal building on this planet, you will step out into bright, diffused daylight without any direct sunlight, and the temperature will be ideal, neither warm nor cold. You will see buildings made of solid gold and silver, and the pebbles on the ground will be precious stones like rubies and pearls. The soil will be white musk, while the grass will be made from saffron, which is the most expensive spice in the world, requiring over seventy thousand flowers to produce just one pound. Everything in heaven will be made from materials that are rare and expensive in this world.

"We shall have removed all ill feeling from their hearts; streams will flow at their feet. They will say, 'Praise be to God, who has guided us to this: had God not guided us, We would never have found the way. The messengers of our Lord brought the Truth.' A voice will call out to them, 'This is the Garden you have been given as your own on account of your deeds.'" (7:43)

The Prophet said that the appetizer at the banquet will be caudate lobe of whale liver, the main course will be beef from a bull that will have grazed on various grasses of heaven, and the drink will be water from a spring called Salsabil.[40] A caudate lobe is a particular part of a liver, and that is what has been specifically mentioned, not the whole liver. Why these foods have been chosen for the first meal hasn't been explained, but it may have something to do with the new bodies that everyone will have and their nutritional requirements. Our new bodies will be pure like those of newborn babies, and the first meal would need to be special.

At this banquet, we will probably meet the ghilman for the first time. They will be beautiful young male servants who have been described as immortal youths who look like scattered pearls. They will greet you as you arrive for the banquet and take you to your reserved seat. Some of them will be preparing meals, while others will be serving at the tables. They will be at your beck and call and will treat you like royalty. Ghilman will be non-humans created in heaven for the service of its human inhabitants, and they will be programmed to serve without hesitation.

In descriptions of banquets in heaven, the Qur'an usually mentions houris as accompanying their husbands, but at this first banquet, we will assume that houri wives will not be present, as we're going to meet them for the first time at our mansions when we arrive there. It is said that, from the time of their creation, they have been living in palaces guarded by angels and have not been allowed any interaction with any human being or jinn until they meet their husbands. Therefore, they're not likely to be present at the welcome banquet for which they would have to travel to a public place, and a banquet will not be the right place for anyone to meet their new spouses for the first time. Not all houris will be wives, however; instead, many will serve as servants, like the ghilman, and it is possible that these will be present at the banquet. If you were reunited with a human spouse, then he or she will, of course, be with you.

Everyone will be seated on luxurious couches, and the ghilman will serve various courses of meals. In addition to the appetizer and main course, there will be fruits in abundance and various drinks from the free-flowing streams of heaven. We will discuss the food and drink of heaven in the next chapter, but there are many types of fruits and four types of drinks that will always be available: water, wine, milk, and honey.

The cutlery and crockery at the table will be of gold or silver, depending on which level of heaven you're in. The glassware will be of silver that will look like crystal, and your drinking cup will constantly be refilled by the ghilman. The couches will be covered with beautiful, soft, and comfortable brocade.

One of the things you'll discover is that you can eat and drink endlessly without ever feeling full. Everything will be digested immediately. You will eat and emit a sweet-smelling perspiration, and the supply of food and drink will be endless. You'll be able to eat as long as you want. The food will taste much better than anything you've ever had in this life, so you'll probably want to eat a lot, especially since there'll be no chance of getting fat or sick from overeating.

At this gathering, you will be with your family and friends whom you met earlier, and you will also socialize with other people. You will notice that you're feeling great, with no sense of anything bad ever having happened to you, and you'll have no negative feelings towards anyone else you meet, even people you didn't like on earth. Everyone will be polite, and there will be no idle talk, gossip, or frivolous chatter, but people will still laugh a lot. The main topic of discussion will be about how happy everyone is at having managed to avoid hell and making it into heaven. People will praise God for having sent them to heaven.

Talking about such an occasion, the Qur'an says, "So God will save them from the woes of that Day, give them radiance and gladness, and reward them, for their steadfastness, with a Garden and silken robes. They will sit on couches, feeling neither scorching heat nor biting cold, with shady [branches] spread above them and clusters of fruit hanging close at hand. They will be served with silver plates and gleaming silver goblets according to their fancy, and they will be given a drink infused with ginger from a stream called Salsabil. Everlasting youths will attend them—if you could see them you would think them scattered pearls—and if you were to look around, you will see bliss and great wealth: they will wear garments of green silk and brocade; they will be adorned with silver bracelets; their Lord will give them a pure drink. [It will be said], 'This is your reward. Your endeavors are appreciated.'" (76:11-22)

A major topic of discussion in heaven, especially when people first arrive, will be how everyone managed to make it to heaven. People will describe their own stories of the path they took in life that led them to where they are now. The Qur'an describes one such conversation. "They will turn to one another with questions: one will say, 'I had a close companion on earth who used to ask me, "Do you really believe that after we die and become dust and bone, we shall be brought for judgment?"' Then he will say, 'Shall we look for him?' He will look down and see him in the midst of the Fire, and say to him, 'By God, you almost brought me to ruin! Had it not been for the grace of my Lord, I too would have been taken to Hell.' Then he will say [to his blessed companions], 'Are we never to die again after our earlier death? Shall we never suffer? This truly is the supreme triumph!'" (37:50-60)

Even though people will now be in heaven, not everyone will be sure about what to expect there, and they'll be asking each other if it's true that they'll never die again. As I mentioned earlier, a lot of people, maybe most, are not familiar with what to expect in heaven, and they will be the ones asking questions. Since you've read this book, maybe you could be one of those explaining to them that, really, there is no death anymore.

Death of Death

When people have finished eating dinner, a drama will be staged that will be broadcast to everyone in both heaven and hell in which a ram representing death will be ceremoniously slaughtered. This will symbolize and drive home into everyone's mind that there will be no more death in the afterlife, either for people in heaven or hell. It will lay to rest any doubts anyone may still have about whether death is a possibility. The people of heaven will be happy beyond belief, and the people of hell will be saddened beyond measure.

The Prophet said, "On the Day of Resurrection death will be brought forward in the shape of a beautiful black and white ram. Then an announcer will call, 'Oh people of paradise!' Thereupon they will stretch their necks and look carefully. The caller will say, 'Do you know this?' They will say, 'Yes, this is death.' By then all of them will have seen it. Then it will be announced again, 'Oh people of hell!' They will stretch their necks and look carefully. The caller will say, 'Do you know this?' They will say, 'Yes, this is death.' And by then all of them will have seen it. Then that ram will be slaughtered and the caller will say, 'Oh people of paradise! Eternity for you and no death, Oh people of hell! Eternity for you and no death.'" Then the Prophet recited the following verse from the Qur'an: "Warn them [Muhammad] of the Day of Remorse when the matter will be decided, for they are heedless and do not believe." (19:38-39) He further said, "If anyone could die from happiness the people of heaven would die at that moment, and if anyone could die from grief the people of hell would die when they hear that."[41]

There are people who say that those in hell will be annihilated at some stage. But this hadith lays that speculation to rest—both heaven and hell are for eternity, and there is no death anymore.

The Qur'an says, "After the one death they will taste death no more. God will guard them from the torment of Hell, a bounty from your Lord. That is the supreme triumph." (44:56-57)

How will people be able to see this spectacle? It will be a lifelike, high-definition, 3-D holographic display. It will appear that the drama is being staged near you, and all the billions of people in heaven and hell will see it simultaneously as if it were occurring nearby. When thinking of heaven, don't think of 10 AD or 610 AD; think 3,000 AD, when such things might be common, and heaven will be much more advanced than that.

Transportation to Your New Home

After your first meal, you will finally be ready to go to your home in heaven and get to see what you're going to receive. In the next chapter, we will see what that might be, but first, we will need to get there. After dinner, we will get into our spacecraft again, and this time, they'll fly us to our mansions in heaven for the first time, where we will also get to meet our new spouses. I can imagine my wife saying when she reads this, "You can't wait to meet the houris, can you?"

7

What You Will Get in Heaven

One day the Prophet said to his Companions, "Who will strive hard with sincerity for paradise? For there is nothing like paradise. By the Lord of the Ka'bah (the center of Muslim worship in Mecca), it is sparkling light, sweet basil waving in the breeze, a lofty palace, a flowing river, abundant ripe fruit, a beautiful wife and many fine garments, in a place of eternal abode, in ease and luxury, in beautiful, strongly built, lofty houses." They said, "We will strive hard for it, oh Messenger of God." He said, "Say, if God wills."[1]

What you will get in heaven will depend on which level and which grade of heaven you've been assigned to. Apart from that, every good action you do in this life produces something extra for you in your assigned home in heaven, and every single person on earth has a home assigned for him or her. I mentioned in Chapter 4 that even a prayer of a few words results in a tree being planted for you and some extra daily prayers taking about ten minutes result in a new mansion being built for you in heaven. Therefore, every single person will get something different.

God himself has described what people in higher levels of heaven will get as being beyond our imagination. Therefore, I will describe what that person will get who will get the absolute least, and since you're unlikely to be that person, you're free to imagine that what you will get will be a lot better.

Moses asked God what would be the least a person would get in heaven and God told him the story of the very last person to enter heaven who will be assigned the lowest rank and get the least amount, and we will relate that story here. When Moses asked God what people of the highest ranks would get, God told him, "They would be blessed with bounties which no eye has seen, no ear has heard and no human mind has perceived." This is in the Hadith[2] as well as in the Bible.[3]

The Qur'an says, "No soul knows what joy is kept hidden in store for them as a reward for what they have done." (32:17)

What people in the highest ranks of heaven will get may be beyond our imagination, but what people of the lowest ranks will get is also absolutely mind-boggling. This is so because God has the ability to create without limit, and he is not bound by any resource constraints, as we are on earth. If God wants to reward someone, he can order things into existence ad infinitum. "He is the Originator of the heavens and the earth, and when He decrees something, He says only, 'Be,' and it is." (2:117)

Some people who are more inclined towards spirituality look askance at descriptions of the materialistic abundance of heaven. The reality of heaven will be that our relationship with God will be more important than any material possessions, but since we will have physical bodies, we will have a mixture of both spiritual and physical pleasures, as we do on earth.

The Last Person to Enter Heaven[4]

On the Day of Judgment, some people will go directly to heaven, but some will go to hell for a while, and after a period of punishment, they will be taken out and transferred to heaven. This process will continue until one last person will be extricated from hell and moved to heaven, and after that, the gates of hell will be shut tight and the remaining people will never get out.

The story of the last person to enter heaven is interesting because, since the last person will get the least, it gives us an idea of the absolute minimum reward that a person will receive in heaven. There are slightly different versions of this story, but I've put them together to create a more complete account.

A companion of the Prophet related hearing this story from the Prophet, who in turn was informed by God that Moses had asked him what would be the least reward a person would get in heaven, and this is what God had told him.

The last person to enter heaven will crawl out of hell and consider himself the luckiest person of all humans. He will be burnt black from the heat of hell and will be alternately crawling on all fours and getting up and walking. Once out of its range, he will turn to hell and say, "Blessed is he who has saved me from you. God has given me something he has not given to any one of those in earlier or later times." He will be imagining that he's the only person who has ever managed to escape from hell.

He will then be in a no-man's-land between heaven and hell. He will see a tree and will say, "Oh my Lord, bring me closer to this tree so that I may enjoy its shade and drink of its water." God will reply, "Oh son of Adam, perhaps if I grant you this, you will ask me for something else?" The man will promise not to ask for anything else and will be brought close to the tree.

Then he will see a second tree better than the first one and will say, "Oh my Lord, bring me near to this tree so that I may drink its water and enjoy its shade, then I will not ask you for anything more."

God will say, "Oh son of Adam, did you not promise me that you would not ask me for anything else? Perhaps if I bring you closer to this tree, you will ask for more?" The man will promise not to ask for anything else, and God will bring him closer to the second tree.

Then a third tree will appear near the gates of paradise, and it will be better than the first two. The man will say, "Oh my Lord, bring me closer to this tree so that I may enjoy its shade and drink its water, and I will not ask for anything more."

God will say, "Oh son of Adam, did you not promise me that you would not ask me for anything more?" He will say, "Yes, my Lord, I will not ask you for anything more." So God will bring him closer to the third tree. When he is brought close, he will hear the voices of the people of Paradise, and will say, "Oh my Lord, admit me into it."

In my view, these trees could actually be different planets, and the man might be moving from one planet to another, finally ending up on the planet we discussed earlier that is the gateway to heaven.

He will then be asked about what he did in this life, and God will say to the angels, "Ask him about his minor sins and conceal his major sins." So, it will be said to him, "You did this and that on this day and that day, and did that on this day and that day." And he will be told, "Against every sin, there is for you a piety." He will exclaim, "Oh Lord, but indeed, I had done things I do not see here!" The narrator remarked that the Prophet laughed till his teeth were visible.[5] The man will be thinking that if all his bad deeds were being converted into rewards, then he might as well remind God of some other sins he had committed that were not being listed.

God will say to him, "Go and enter paradise." He will go to it, but he will imagine that it is already full, and he will return and say, "Oh Lord, I have found it full." He will be told three times to enter heaven, and each time he'll come back saying it is full.

God will say, "Oh son of Adam, what do you want me to give you so that you will never ask me for anything else? Do you remember the time you were in hell?" He will say, "Yes." It will be said to him, "Wish for whatever you want." The man will give a list of things he would like, and God will grant him everything. Then, once the man has run out of things to ask for, God will remind him of additional things and grant him those. Then God will say, "I grant you all that and as much again, and as much again…" until after the fifth time, the man will say, "Stop, that's enough." Then God will say, "You will get all that and ten times as much."[6]

In another version of the story, God will say, "Go and enter paradise, and you will have what equals the world and ten times as much."[7]

He will say, "Oh my Lord, are you making fun of me when you are the Lord of the Worlds?"

The narrator laughed and said, "Why do you not ask me why I am laughing?" They asked, "Why are you laughing?" He said, "Because the Messenger of God laughed and they asked him, 'Why are you laughing, oh Messenger of God?'"

The Prophet replied, "Because the Lord of the Worlds will laugh when he is asked, 'Are you making fun of me when you are the Lord of the Worlds?' God will say, 'I am not making fun of you, but I am able to do whatever I wish.'"[8]

So, the man to get the least reward in heaven will get ten times as much as what this whole earth contains, and that's why it is said that what the people in the higher ranks of heaven will get will be, "Bounties which no eye has seen, no ear has heard and no human mind has perceived."

The man will be burnt black from the fire of hell, so he will be made to swim in the River of Life outside the gates of heaven and will come out with a brand-new body and will be dressed in new clothes. Then he will pass through the gates of heaven and will see a being of great presence and beauty and will start bowing down to him. The being will say, "Why are you bowing?" and the man will reply, "Because I thought you were God."[9]

He will say, "Get up, I'm not God, I'm your servant coming to receive you. You have thousands of other servants like me." According to one hadith, the lowest person in heaven will get eighty thousand ghilman as servants, and this was probably a ghilman he just met.

They will then proceed towards his mansion, and the man will see something emitting huge amounts of light, and he will start to bow down again and the ghilman will say, "Why are you bowing?" and he will say, "Isn't that God?" The ghilman will tell him that the light is coming from his mansion that is lit up with intense illumination. As he will get nearer, he will see an absolutely enormous mansion towering over them that will be many miles long on each side and that is larger than any structure on earth. It will be made from a single hollow pearl and will be studded with jewels like emeralds, diamonds, rubies, etc.

The grounds surrounding the mansion will be lush, green meadows stretching as far as the eyes can see, with streams flowing, and full of fruit trees and flowers.

The air will smell of perfume. The soil will be made of saffron, and the ground will be littered with pebbles of precious stones like pearls, rubies, and diamonds.

The man will enter the mansion and will be met by two stunningly beautiful houris who will be his wives. They will say to him, "Praise be to God who has created you for us and created us for you."[10] He will be struck speechless and will stare at one of them for a long time.

This is a man who has just come out of hell, which he probably remembers very clearly, and on earth he couldn't have imagined even a king having such riches, and here he is with all this, and it may take a while for him to get used to things.

On inspection, he will find that the land he's been given is so vast that it will take him a thousand years to explore it all.[11] And the mansion he would have just seen will turn out to be one of many belonging to him that will be scattered throughout his territory.

His words will be, "No one has ever been given anything like what I have been given." Little will he know that this is the least that anyone will receive.

Territory

The least territory a person will get has been variously described as ten times the size of earth, or equal to a thousand years' journey. Since travel time in those days was on camels, we can calculate how much a person will need to travel to explore all his personal property.

At an average pace, a camel covers twenty-five miles in a day, which is equal to about nine thousand miles in a year. In one thousand years, it will have traveled nine million miles. So if you're crisscrossing your private land to explore it, you could travel millions of miles before you see all of it, equivalent to traveling three hundred and seventy-five times around the earth. And that is assuming that the speed of travel referred to was at the pace of a camel. It may even be that whatever speed you travel at, it will take a thousand years to see everything you own.

It is likely that your territory will be a single planet that will be at least ten times the size of this earth. All of it will belong to you alone, and you'll be living there with your spouse and servants. On this land, you will have many mansions scattered about and you'll be able to travel from one to the next.

Every person will live on their own, unless they're married to a fellow human being instead of a houri or ghilman. If you have a human spouse, then you'll be sharing the same home; otherwise everyone will have their own territory, and family and friends will travel to meet each other.

To travel in your land, you'll require some form of vehicles, and I believe they will be aircraft, and for traveling to visit family and friends on other planets, you'll be using spaceships. As we discussed earlier, you're likely to have a fleet of these for various purposes.

What we're talking about up to now is for people of the lowest ranks in heaven, while people in the higher levels will have a whole lot more—clusters of planets, or maybe even whole galaxies. It might take them millions of years to discover all of what they own.

Mansions

Because there are so many grades in heaven, it's not always easy to figure out what grade something that's been mentioned belongs to. In some cases, it's been specified that a certain reward is for someone in a particular level, but when it's not been made clear, we're left to figure it out ourselves.

If I describe a certain size house, and your house turns out to be smaller when you get there, I hope you won't hold it against me. For one thing, you can't have negative thoughts in heaven, but what I can say with certainty is that whatever you will be given even in the lowest grade will be so fabulously beyond anything you're capable of imagining that it won't really matter if I'm wrong. You'll be happy with what you get. I'm going by what the Qur'an and Hadith have said and not exaggerating, because the highest levels of heaven hold unimaginable rewards, but something I describe may belong to a higher grade than where you may go to; therefore, some uncertainty arises from not knowing what grade a particular reward belongs to. I'm clarifying this point because the house I'm about to describe is beyond imagination.

According to the Prophet, there will be a house in heaven that will be built from a single hollowed pearl that will be sixty miles (almost one hundred kilometers) in diameter.[12]

Assuming that it's carved out of a sphere that's been sliced in half, this house would be sixty miles in length and thirty miles high.[13]

The Qur'an mentions tall, multi-storied buildings, "But those who are mindful of their Lord will have lofty dwellings built for them, one above the other, graced with flowing streams. This is a promise from God: God does not break His promise." (39:20)

Compare a house thirty miles high to a present-day skyscraper. It will be one hundred times taller than the Empire State Building, or six times the height of Mount Everest. If it has ceiling heights of one thousand feet (compared to the usual eight to ten feet), it will have one hundred and sixty floors, with each floor being as tall as a hundred-story building.

Being a different universe, everything will be bigger in heaven, including human bodies, so let's assume that the sizes mentioned are dimensions of a house in heaven if it were transported to earth. To get an idea of the different scales of measurement in heaven, we'll use the size that the Prophet said humans would be. He said that people would be ninety feet tall, which is roughly sixteen times taller than the average human height of five-and-a-half feet.

Since our size will be bigger in heaven, something that is sixteen feet in height on earth will seem like one foot tall in heaven. In that case, a ceiling height of one thousand feet in earthly measurement will actually feel sixteen times shorter, or sixty-two feet, which is still a lot higher than the usual eight to ten feet ceiling heights in normal houses. Ceiling heights of sixty-two feet will be equivalent to a six-story building.

Just the ground floor of such a building in heaven will be almost eighty billion square feet, without even counting all one hundred and sixty floors. Dividing by sixteen will make it feel like five billion square feet, and then counting all one hundred and sixty floors, with decreasing square footage as you go up because of the dome-like shape of the house, makes it four hundred billion square feet.

If we add up the size of every single home in the United States, the result would be about three hundred billion square feet. The house in heaven will have more square footage than all the houses in America combined. And all of this will be for one person.

The house will be carved out of a single pearl and will be inlaid with other precious stones, such as rubies, emeralds, diamonds, etc.

That should put in perspective what we're talking about when we're discussing heaven. It is totally out of proportion to anything we would have imagined if we were just speculating about it ourselves, but I'm going by figures from authentic texts, which I believe to be true. What I cannot say is which grade in heaven you will need to be in to get a house of this magnitude. And since people will have more than one home, some people might get many houses like this.

As if a house of this size were not large enough, another one has been mentioned made of pearls, aquamarine, and rubies that will be over twelve hundred miles in size—that's over two thousand kilometers.[14]

The Prophet also mentioned houses that will be translucent and you'll be able to see the outside from the interior and also be able to look inside while you're outside the house.[15] The idea of transparent houses would have seemed pretty incredible for people living fourteen hundred years ago, but today we're familiar with glass. The difference will be that these mansions will be made from translucent emeralds and other gems, not glass.

A variation of this hadith is that instead of the whole house being translucent, it will have transparent windowpanes made of precious stones.

According to one account, the house of emerald will have many red rooms and each of those will have green sub-rooms, adding up to thousands of rooms.

At another time, the Prophet mentioned houses made out of alternating bricks of solid gold and silver with mortar of musk. Musk is a rare substance that is used to make perfume. The bricks of solid gold and silver will be the least precious material that any house will be made from. There will be no bricks of the type we have in this world.

Regardless of how large a mansion you will get, you will find that you will know your way around it better than you know your way around your own home in this world, and everything will feel familiar to you. The feeling of strangeness that you get when you move into a new house will not be there. The moment you enter your mansion in heaven, it will feel like you've lived there all your life, and you'll be able to find your way around it without any problem. This information will be programmed into your brain.

The house will be surrounded with lush, beautifully landscaped gardens that will be irrigated with water from underground channels. The Qur'an says, "God has promised the believers, both men and women, Gardens graced with flowing streams where they will remain; good, peaceful homes in Gardens of lasting bliss." (9:72) Although this translation of the Qur'an mentions "Gardens graced with flowing streams," other translations render it as "Gardens underneath which rivers flow." I take this to mean that the mansions and gardens will be irrigated with water from underground channels, which could be underground piping like we have today. The idea is that the vegetation will not rely on rain, but will be irrigated with underground water.

There will be thousands of rooms of different colors in the house. Red and green rooms have been mentioned, and many of them will have a throne for the owner, while other rooms will have tables laid with countless varieties of food. The occupant of the house will be like a king (or queen), and when he enters a room, he will sit on his throne, with ghilman attending to his every need.[16]

Like everything in heaven, houses will be built to last eternally, and they will be maintenance-free. It is said that these houses, despite their gigantic sizes, will not have a single crack or imperfection. The environment in heaven will not be corrosive like on earth, where a house starts deteriorating the day it is built. There will be no rainstorms, dust, or termites. There will be no sewerage lines required, since there will be no toilets. The climate in heaven will always be perfect and insect-free, so windows could be kept open at all times. It will always be daylight outside, so illumination could also come from windows. It has been mentioned that if someone would like some darkness, they would be able to draw the curtains.

If any work needs to be done, such as rearranging the décor once in a while, it will be done by the ghilman. With at least eighty thousand ghilman to serve you, you'll never have to do any work yourself.

Even though these mansions in heaven sound so fabulous to us, they seem to be very easy for God to create. The Prophet mentioned various acts of worship, taking only a few minutes each, that we can do to create a new house in heaven for ourselves.[17] In this way, some people may have accumulated several of these houses.

In recent years, scientists have been finding evidence that some dead stars, known as white dwarfs, have cores made out of diamonds that are thousands of miles in diameter. So that's one confirmed way for the formation of gemstones of enormous size. In heaven, these might be transported to a location and have houses carved out of them.

Marriage and Sex

Humans are preprogrammed to be attracted to members of the opposite sex, and this trait is so strong that it's even visible in children. Since our natures will be the same in heaven, one of the rewards we have been promised are spouses of the opposite sex for companionship. As to the question of whether there will be sex in heaven, the answer is yes, and we will also discuss that.

If we go back to the story of Adam, he was living in heaven and he had everything that he could have wished for, but God created Eve for him as a companion, which suggests that life even in heaven is incomplete without everyone having at least one companion of the opposite sex.

The Prophet said that every single person in heaven will be married.[18] Some people will be married to fellow human beings, and some will be married to houris or ghilman. Some may possibly have a mix of both human and nonhuman spouses. For example, a man may have a human wife and also houris. There's no concept of same-sex marriage in heaven, so please don't even ask.

According to the Qur'an, "They will have pure spouses and there they will stay." (2:25) "Their Lord will give those who are mindful of God Gardens graced with flowing streams, where they will stay with pure spouses and God's good pleasure." (3:15)

Most of the time, the Qur'an is gender neutral and refers to marriage partners as spouses or companions, rather than husbands or wives. This way it is clear that the

Qur'an refers to both men and women in heaven being married.

Since men are eager for houris, it has also been made clear that they will get them. "We shall wed them to maidens with large, dark eyes." (44:54) However, most translations of the Qur'an, instead of saying "wed them to maidens," say "wed them to companions," in which case the verse would apply to both men and women—they'll all be wed to fair companions with large, dark eyes.

For men, it is stated in a hadith that the minimum number of wives will be two.[19] While no figure has been given for women, it is assumed that they will have one husband each.

One of the most frequent questions women ask is that if men will be getting houris, what will they be getting. The answer is that a woman will either be married to a human husband, which could be the same husband that she had in this life, or if she was not married and no men are available, she will have a special ghilman created for her, who will be the perfect husband of her dreams.

On one online forum, I read a comment by a Muslim lady in which she complained that by removing all feelings of jealousy, God would be brainwashing women into accepting their husbands' having more than one wife, which she thought was unfair. She also resented that only men would be allowed multiple spouses.

Regarding the question of why men will get two or more wives, while women will get only one husband, the answer is that, first of all, we don't know exactly if women will get one husband or more, since it's not been clearly stated. Even if they were to get more than one husband, it would probably not be mentioned because it would be considered a bit scandalous by some people. The most frequent reason given for women getting one husband is that women's nature is such that they're happiest with one man.

Let women wait until they get there to find out if they'll get only one husband or more. While it may be possible in this world to feel disgruntled about something someone may tell you about heaven, no such feelings will exist once you're actually there. Not only will you get rewarded beyond anything you expect, or would have earned, but, in addition, God himself will regularly ask you if there's anything else you would like. So you'll be able to ask for anything you want.

People will live in their mansions with their spouses and servants. Their spouses will be their closest companions and will usually accompany them on their trips, except on the regular trips to meet God, when the non-human spouses will stay at home. This is surmised from the hadith about the meeting with God, which states that when a person will come back home from their trip, their houri (or ghilman) spouse will say that they look even more beautiful than when they left, and they will say the same thing to their spouse.[20]

People will be married to their partners in heaven. There will be sex between them. It is made very clear in the Hadith that there is sex in heaven. Even some fairly intimate details have been described, such as that there will be no flow of bodily fluids during the sex act, and there will be no pregnancies, since there will be no procreation, and sex will be purely for pleasure. Women will remain virgins after sex. Both men and women will have the capacity for having sex for long periods of time without getting tired or feeling any discomfort. Men will be able to perform the sex act with as many wives as they have without running out of energy.[21]

In this world, sex by itself is not a sin as long as it's indulged in within the bounds of law, which means that it's with someone you're married to. Beyond that, sex can cause harm and is forbidden. It can cause jealousy, disease, broken relationships, unwanted pregnancies, and many other types of harm. If these negative consequences are removed, then you're left with something that is good and enjoyable, and that's what heaven will have. This will be just like everything else in heaven, where harmful consequences will have been removed, such as being able to eat lots of food without suffering any associated problems. In this world, if you overeat, you will suffer from indigestion, visits to the bathroom, weight gain, potential diseases, and so on, but in heaven, you'll be able to eat non-stop for as long as you like. Similarly, you'll be able to have sex for as long as you like.

If you were married in this world and your spouse also makes it to heaven, then you will be married to him or her in heaven as well. You will meet before the time of entering heaven and will be told, "Enter Paradise, you and your spouses: you will be filled with joy." (43:70)

If a man was married to more than one woman, he'll be able to have all of them, if they themselves agree to be with him. This is assumed, though there's no specific hadith stating this.

If a woman was married to more than one man and all of them go to heaven, then she will be given the choice of which one she would like to be with, and she will choose the man who treated her best or is in the highest rank in heaven. There is another opinion that states that she will be with the last man she was married to in this world, and this is considered to be the most correct view.[22]

If one of the spouses earns a place in a higher grade, then the other one will be upgraded to the higher level as well, so that they can both be together.

If a person was not married in this life, they will still be married to someone in heaven. If there are no humans left, then they'll be married to houris or ghilman. There will be no instance where someone will be left alone without a spouse.

With all negativity removed from their souls, and everyone having beautiful bodies and enjoying fabulous luxuries, relationships will be as perfect as everything else in heaven. Husbands and wives will love each other and compliment each other on every occasion, and they will never tire of each other. It has been said that every time they even look away from their partner for a moment and then look back, they will feel that their spouse has grown in beauty. Whether they will be actually increasing in beauty is uncertain, but it will certainly appear like that to them.

Having your husband or wife from this world with you in heaven gives a whole new meaning to the phrase 'eternal love.' If you both live a good life and both make it to heaven, then you will be together for eternity. Any flaws you see in each other now will be gone, and both of you will be perfect in character and physical beauty.

Since humans will be superior to houris and ghilman, being married to a fellow human will be considered better than having houris or ghilman as spouses. Women from earth will be even more ravishingly beautiful than the houris, so no matter what your wife may look like here, in heaven she will be a woman of astonishing beauty. The same applies to husbands.

The man will be the king of the household, and it will be the woman who will be the queen, no matter how many houris and ghilman there are.

There will be no pregnancies in heaven and no childbirth.[23] Females, human or houri, will most likely not have the body parts required for conceiving. But if someone asks for a child as a special request to God, the Prophet said that maybe a special houri would conceive and give birth to a baby, and it would grow up to the required age, all in a matter of one hour.[24] Since God will fulfill every wish, a request for a baby will also be granted, but it won't be the norm. According to one opinion, although every wish will be granted, there will be some things people will not ask for.

One day, when I was telling my brother about houris and ghilman, he asked if they would be "androids," which are robots that look like humans. My sister-in-law, who was present at the time, said that she wouldn't want an android as a husband. But the houris and ghilman will be so human-like that you probably would not be able to tell them apart from humans in any way. They will look human, act human, have feelings, intellect, humor, and everything else that humans have, so I think everyone will love them. Personally, if someone doesn't want their houris, I'll be happy to take them.

Servants

We have previously described ghilman as human-like beings that are handsome, beautifully dressed, eternal youths who look like scattered pearls. They're a special creation of God made for the service of the inhabitants of heaven. The Prophet said that the least person in heaven would get eighty thousand ghilman as servants.[25]

If people in the lowest level will get so many, then it would be fair to speculate that people in the higher levels will get millions.

In another hadith it's been mentioned that each woman in heaven will get seventy thousand male ghilman and seventy thousand female houris as servants.[26] Some special houris and ghilman will be spouses for people in heaven, while there will be thousands more who will be servants.

They will be everywhere you go on your realm, taking care of your mansions, preparing your food, serving you meals, bringing your clothes, helping you change, and so on. They will be at your beck and call everywhere you go, unless you want to be left alone. If you want to be with your spouse for some intimacy, the ghilman and houri servants will go away and leave you alone.

Food

Our bodies in heaven will be totally different, able to eat to our heart's content without any negative consequences, and there will be immense varieties and quantities of food and drink available.[27]

Among foods, fruits are mentioned the most in the Qur'an. "[Prophet], give those who believe and do good works the news that they will have Gardens graced with flowing streams. Whenever they are given sustenance from the fruits of these Gardens, they will say, 'We have been given this before,' because they were provided with something like it." (2:25) Fruits in heaven will be similar to the fruits of earth and will seem familiar, but they will be vastly superior in size, texture, smell, and taste.

It has been said that there will be endless varieties of food in heaven, many of which will remind us of foods in this world, but many that will be new to us. Even those foods that resemble ones we have eaten here will be superior in every way.

While only a few fruits have been mentioned in the Qur'an—dates, grapes, pomegranates, and figs—it talks about many varieties of fruits being available. "For those who fear [the time when they will] stand before their Lord there are two gardens." (55:46) "With every kind of fruit in pairs." (55:52) "But those who took heed of God will enjoy cool shade, springs, and any fruits they desire; [they will be told], 'Eat and drink to your hearts' content as a reward for your deeds.'" (77:41)

Gardens in heaven will be full of trees with low-hanging fruits always within easy reach. When you're sitting or lying down and would like to have a fruit, it will come to you without your having to make any effort.[28] Either a ghilman will bring it to you or it will automatically materialize in your hand. As soon as a fruit is taken from a tree, a new one will grow immediately to replace it. The supply of fruit will be all year round with no seasonal variation.

Someone asked, "Oh Prophet! Are there dates in the Garden? Because I love dates." And the Prophet replied: "Yes, there are dates... the dates of the Garden have golden branches. They have golden shoots. They have leaves as beautiful as the finest clothing anyone has ever seen. There are golden bunches of dates. Even the stalks of these bunches of dates are of gold. At the base of each golden date are sticky scales. They have fruits like giant jars, softer than foam, sweeter than honey."[29]

There are some hints that every tree will have many varieties of fruits growing on it, and the fruit a person feels like having is the one he'll get. It is possible that each tree in heaven will have the ability to produce any fruit that is desired.[30]

Meat has also been mentioned in the Qur'an. "We provide them with any fruit or meat they desire." (52:22)

"[There will be] any fruit they choose; the meat of any bird they like." (56:20-21)

We've already mentioned fish liver and beef being on the menu for the first meal in heaven. There is a hadith according to which, if a person sees a bird flying in the air and wishes to eat it, an angel will immediately present it to him fully roasted.[31] After he finishes eating, the bones of the bird will reassemble, and it will fly away.[32] Obviously, the laws of nature are very different in heaven, and what might be considered miraculous in this world will be common there.

Although I can't find the relevant hadith to back this up, when I was young, I was told that in heaven anything you wish for will appear in your hand. It's as though you won't have to turn to an angel or ghilman to ask for something; your thoughts will be read and your wishes complied with.

At every meal in your own mansion, you will be served a vast array of maybe a hundred or more dishes by the ghilman. There will a wide variety of cooked dishes, including breads, meats and desserts. At public receptions, there could be thousands of different dishes.

With so much food available, the best part will be that your body will be capable of eating for as long as you like and the food will continuously be digested and emitted as a sweet-smelling sweat, so you'll be able to try all the dishes without ever feeling full or bloated.

Drinks

There are four types of drinks that have been mentioned in the Qur'an that will flow like rivers and will be available everywhere all the time. These are water, wine, milk, and honey. "Here is a picture of the Garden promised to the pious: rivers of water forever pure, rivers of milk forever fresh, rivers of wine, a delight for those who drink, rivers of honey clarified and pure, [all] flow in it; there they will find fruit of every kind; and they will find forgiveness from their Lord." (47:15)

All these drinks will be of much better quality than in this world and will never get spoiled or contaminated in any way and will not have any negative consequences that drinking these beverages may have in this world. Water will remain pure, milk will not spoil nor be hard to digest for anyone, honey will be clear, and wine will not cause intoxication or headache.

My own interpretation is that these drinks will be piped in and available on tap in every home, like water connections that we have now. That makes more sense than to imagine actual rivers of these drinks flowing outside your home. It'll be great having water, wine, milk, and honey on tap and not having to go out and get them in cartons or bottles.

There is a river called Kauthar, which means "abundance," that was gifted by God to Prophet Muhammad. "We have truly given abundance to you [Prophet]." (108:1) This is interpreted to mean that abundance in general was given to the Prophet, but it is also the name of a specific river that is said to have banks of gold, a bed of rubies and pearls, and soil of musk, and whose water is whiter than milk and sweeter than honey.[33] On its banks will be scattered millions of cups for people to drink from, and tents, or houses, of hollowed pearls for people to stay in. Water from this river will flow outside the gates of heaven to the Cistern of Kauthar, where people will drink its water before entering heaven. The river will also flow in heaven and will have large long-necked birds drinking its water.[34]

Another spring that has been mentioned in the Qur'an is Salsabil. "They will be served with silver plates and gleaming silver goblets according to their fancy, and they will be given a drink infused with ginger from a spring called Salsabil." (76:15-18) This will be the drink served at the first meal in heaven.

There is also a spring called Tasnim, which means "opulence." "They will be served a sealed nectar, its seal [perfumed with] a fragrant herb—let those who strive,

strive for this—mixed with the water of Tasnim, a spring from which those brought near will drink." (83:25-28) "Those brought near" refers to people in the upper levels of heaven.

The Qur'an also mentions that "The righteous will have a drink mixed with kafur [camphor, a fragrant herb], a spring for God's servants, which flows abundantly at their wish." (76:5-6)

Apart from the various drinks that have been mentioned, it is fair to say that there will be countless varieties of drinks. Since wine will be available, there could be infinite varieties of wine, just as there will be different flavors of water, milk, and honey. As with food, we will be able to drink endlessly, and the excess fluids will continuously be emitted as fragrant sweat.

The drinks in heaven will taste a lot better than what we have now. Even plain water in heaven is said to taste sweeter than honey.

Rivers of Heaven

Most times that heaven is mentioned in the Qur'an, it is described as consisting of gardens with rivers flowing underneath them. This expression is used forty times. Some translations render this as, "Gardens underneath which rivers flow." Others use the expression "Gardens through which rivers flow," while the translation I am using describes it as "Gardens graced with flowing streams." Whichever translation we use, it is clear that the most common image of heaven in the Qur'an is of verdant gardens and flowing streams.

One thing in common between this universe and the new universe is that water is an essential ingredient for sustaining life. The Qur'an says, "Are the disbelievers not aware that the heavens and the earth used to be joined together and that We ripped them apart, that We made every living thing from water? Will they not believe?" (21:30) Life in this universe is made from water and so will it be in heaven.

The Prophet said that there are four rivers of water that emanate from the Throne of God and flow around the existing universe.[35] In the new universe also, water will be the basis for life, and rivers will flow all over heaven. The source of the rivers is said to be the Throne of God, and water will be transported around the new universe to millions of planets. Water on earth is supposed to have been transported here by comets and meteoroids, so there's a scientific basis for the concept of water being distributed around the universe.

We have already mentioned the four rivers of heaven that will consist of water, wine, milk, and honey, and these drinks will be available everywhere. The Prophet said that there will be oceans in heaven holding these beverages, and from there they will flow out like rivers, and be available to everyone.

Descriptions of heaven in the Qur'an repeatedly mention that everything in heaven will be watered with rivers and streams, many of which will flow underground. Depending on the translation used, the Qur'an mentions dozens of times that heaven will have gardens and mansions with rivers flowing underneath them.

I think that there will be many rivers on the surface of heaven, but there will also be underground channels that will water the gardens, such as we have with irrigated lawns. This will be a substitute for rain as a means of watering the vegetation in heaven.

In one hadith, there is mention of a moist, fragrant breeze in heaven, but no mention of regular rainfall, which leads me to believe that heaven will be watered with surface and underground water channels rather than rain.

Geography of Heaven

Heaven will consist of millions, if not billions, of planets. Since the least person will be getting territory ten times the size of this earth, it is fair to assume that everyone will be getting whole planets to themselves, with some people in the highest levels possibly getting thousands or even millions of planets.

The Arabic word for heaven, *jannah*, means something that is hidden from view but is normally used to refer to a garden. The word "paradise" also means garden, and is derived from an ancient Persian word for garden.

Descriptions of heaven in the Qur'an and Hadith describe lush green gardens watered with rivers and streams and full of fruit trees and flowers, with birds flying around feeding on the fruits and rivers of heaven.

It can therefore be surmised that all the planets in heaven will be made up of verdant green landscapes with rivers and streams flowing both on the surface and underground to water the vegetation.

The soil and rocks of these planets will be very different compared to earth, as the soil will be made of saffron, which is a very rare and precious commodity, requiring seventy thousand flowers to make just one pound. In heaven, all the soil will be made of saffron and partly from musk. Musk is also a rare and expensive substance that comes from musk deer and is used to make perfume.

In *Hadi al-arwah*, Ibn Qayyim clarifies the point about the soil of heaven being made from both saffron and musk by saying that the soil will be made from white powdered musk, and the grass will be saffron.[36]

Someone asked the Prophet, "What is paradise made of?" He said, "A brick of silver and a brick of gold and its mortar is musk, strong in scent, and its pebbles are pearls and rubies, and its soil is saffron."[37] The rocks and pebbles on the ground will be precious stones, such as pearls, rubies, and emeralds, which means that any rock formations, such as hills or mountains, will also be made of precious rocks.

It is said that some of the mansions in heaven will be carved out of single pieces of pearls and emeralds, which reinforces the view that rocks in heaven will be made from precious materials. Other mansions will be made from bricks of solid gold and silver, which implies that gold and silver will be very common materials found on the planets in heaven.

There are unlikely to be any deserts or desolate landscapes anywhere, but there will probably be large bodies of water, such as oceans, seas, and lakes. Whales have already been mentioned as a food item, so there will have to be oceans for them to live in.

Mountains have not been mentioned anywhere, but that doesn't mean that there won't be any. Mountainous landscapes on earth are beautiful and people love them; therefore, there will definitely be huge mountains in heaven, and most probably there will also be mansions on the mountaintops. I would personally love a mountainous landscape as the location for my mansion, rather than a flat plain.

Basically if you can imagine something beautiful, then it will be there in heaven, and it will be far better than whatever you can think of. If you want snow-covered mountains, then either they'll already be there or they'll be created for you. Keep in mind that God will be regularly asking you if there's anything more you would like, so you'll be able to ask for whatever you want. I plan to ask for mountains if I don't see any.

The biology of heaven will be very different from that of earth. All the trees will have trunks made from gold, instead of wood.[38] Leaves will be beautiful and feel like silk cloth and be soft to the touch. Each tree will have many types of fruits, and when a fruit is picked, a new one will grow immediately.[39]

The Prophet said that there's a tree in heaven, called the Tree of Tooba, that is so large that a rider could ride in its shade for a hundred years without crossing it.[40] If you were riding a horse at twenty miles per hour, you would cover a distance of seventeen-and-a-half million miles in that time. That would make the tree more than seven hundred times the circumference of earth. We'll divide those numbers by sixteen to account for our larger size, and that still gives us a distance of over a million miles.

Trying to imagine this tree, we could presume that there might be some extremely large planetary bodies, perhaps millions of times bigger than earth. On one of these planets, there could be at least one very large tree, or tree-like structure, with branches extending over a million miles. We've already mentioned houses of gigantic size, so there's no reason why there shouldn't be very large planets and trees as well.

Stretching our imagination a bit, perhaps the Tree of Tooba won't be a regular tree at all; instead, it could be a mushroom-shaped raised platform, with a city on top.

Like humans, who will have very different bodies, animals in heaven will likely have different bodies too. They will probably have no droppings and will not procreate as do the animals we have now. They will feed on fruits, but will not have life cycles similar to animals on earth, and neither will the vegetation depend on the animals for fertilizer or for spreading its seeds.

So much of the geology and biology of earth depends on the life and death cycles of animals, and everything is in a constant state of flux and change. Animals that die in the sea end up forming limestone on the seabed, and then those limestone formations end up on top of mountains when tectonic plates push up the sea floor to form mountains. The top of Mount Everest consists of limestone that came from the bottom of an ocean.

That kind of geology and biology will not exist in heaven. There, the planets will be made to last forever; therefore, all the laws of nature will be totally different.

For one thing, there won't be animals dying and forming rocks. There will be no earthquakes or volcanic eruptions and no plate tectonics. There will be no hurricanes, storms, or tsunamis. In fact, there may be little or no rain.

Basically, there will be no evolution. A planet in heaven will likely be built like a machine with every part in a stable condition and functioning optimally. Once it's been built, it will remain in exactly the same condition forever. Even things that lead to machines breaking down on earth will not exist—like rust, or dirt, or pollution. In heaven, even the atomic structure of elements is likely to be much more stable than on earth, where elements break down at the subatomic level.

Heaven will be different from this earth right down to its atoms and the way elements behave. The new universe will be built on totally different laws of physics compared to this one.

The Prophet mentioned many things being made out of light or emitting light. For example, chairs made from light, gems that shine brightly, and so on. It is possible that everything in heaven will either be made from light or will glow by itself. The whole planet that you'll be living on will be shining brilliantly. The Prophet said that people of higher ranks will appear like stars, so the planets they will be on will appear to be lit up. Since we've been told that planets will not be getting their light from a sun-like star, we can presume that each planet will produce its own light, apart from the light coming from the Throne of God.

If we look at nighttime satellite images of earth, we can see some cities and whole countries glowing with light, while most parts are dark. A satellite image of a planet in heaven is likely to show the whole planet shining brilliantly with no dark spots.

Think of a vastly superior intelligence, which is God, creating a perfect environment with science that is millions of years ahead of what we have now. That's what heaven will be like. This whole universe is made from ancient technology compared to the new one. In evolutionary terms, you could say that this universe is as prehistoric as an amoeba is compared to a human being.

Weather

The temperature in heaven will either be fixed or will fluctuate within a very narrow band that we will find comfortable. The Qur'an says, "They will sit on couches, feeling neither scorching heat nor biting cold, with shady [branches] spread above them and clusters of fruit hanging close at hand." (76:13-14) My interpretation of this verse is that there will be some temperature variation, but it won't ever get uncomfortably hot or cold.

There will be no night-and-day cycle in heaven, and there will be no sun. There will be perpetual daylight that will emanate from the Throne of God located in the center of heaven. The light will be all-pervasive and will illuminate everything without overheating anything, and the planets will probably be lit up on all sides, without having to rotate as earth does.

Cool winds will blow in heaven, laden with clouds and perfumed moisture, but there is no mention of rain like we have on earth. Since planets will be watered with rivers and streams flowing on the surface and underground, rain will not be needed for vegetation.

There is no possibility of adverse weather conditions, such as storms, tornados, and tsunamis. The weather will always be pleasant, but will most likely have enough variation to keep things interesting.

Time

Although there will be no day-and-night cycle in heaven, time will be kept by periodic flashes of extra-bright light that will come from the original light source, which is the Throne of God. This way, people will be able to keep track of the passing of time and be able to calculate future dates for appointments and special occasions.[41]

One of the biggest gifts of heaven will be an eternal life with unlimited time to do everything you ever wanted to do. You will also find that time itself flows at a different rate compared to earth, although you may not notice any difference.

In this life, shortage of time is one of the biggest resource constraints we have. On any given day, a major chunk of our time is spent sleeping, eating, dressing, driving, and so on, and we get only a few hours to do productive work. If you deduct the hours spent working for a living, then we're left with very little time for doing things we enjoy, such as spending time with the family, watching TV, reading books, sports, going on vacations, and so on. I'm sure all of us have a list of things we would do if only we had more time.

In heaven, you'll have unlimited time to do everything you've always wanted to do. For a start, you won't have to sleep or work for a living, so that will free up a lot of time. Secondly, you'll have an unlimited lifespan to accomplish everything you ever wanted to do, and also to plan and achieve new goals that you might think of while you are there.

On a different topic related to time, there are some curious hadiths based on secondary sources that describe how some simple activities will take extraordinary lengths of time. For example, in one case it is said that when a man enters heaven and meets his houri wife for the first time, he will stare at her for forty years.[42] In another place, it is said that a person will recline on his couch for seventy years without changing position.[43] I want to address this issue so that people can make sense of it.

With the laws of nature being different in the new universe, the flow of time will also be different. Normally, if you see a stunningly beautiful woman, you may stare at her for five minutes before saying something or looking away. Even five minutes may be too long, but let's assume that's the case.

What might happen is that what will feels like five minutes in heaven will seem like forty years on earth, meaning that time itself will flow about four million times slower in heaven compared to earth. If an observer went to heaven and were thinking and moving around based on earthly time, then he would need to wait eight years for one minute to pass in heaven. Movement would be so slow that everything will appear frozen in time. But for someone living there, one minute will feel just like one minute feels to us. It is just one of the ways heaven will be different from earth.

Interests and Passions

Once you're in heaven, you will discover that you will remember your life on earth in great detail and have the same personality, interests, and passions that you previously had.

In Chapter 11, I will mention a hadith about a farmer asking God to allow him to plant a field and that the crop will grow and ripen instantly, which shows that people will carry over their interests into heaven.

If a man was a basketball player in this life, then it can be expected that one of the first things he will do when he gets to his house in heaven will be to build a basketball court and start playing with the ghilman.

If you're interested in cars, you'll still be interested in cars in heaven, and you'll be able to collect thousands of the most exotic models that you used to dream about. You could make a list of all the cars you want, and at the next meeting with God, you could give him the list and by the time you arrive back home, you would find a huge, new, thousand-car garage with all the cars you requested sitting there.

If you're interested in fashion and dcsign, then you'll find such an infinite variety of clothes and jewelry of the highest quality that you could spend ages just studying and admiring them.

Once people settle down after arriving in heaven, they're likely to start organizing themselves into the same sort of clubs, organizations, and interest groups that they belonged to before, and you'll have a wide assortment of groups to join, or you could start one yourself.

Do not think of heaven as a totally sterilized and mechanical place that is so perfect and uniform that everyone is alike and everyone loves everyone else equally. You're likely to find that it is a very human and normal place, where you would like some people more than others, enjoy some activities more than others, and so on. You may find that you don't dislike or hate anyone or anything, but you like some people, and enjoy certain activities, more than others.

Fragrance of Heaven

The whole of heaven will be filled with fragrance. Beautiful scents will pervade the atmosphere, and everywhere you go, you'll be encountering new aromas.

To start, your hair, your body, and your clothes will be perfumed. Even your sweat will smell wonderful. It has been mentioned that people will wear many layers of clothes, and each layer will have a different scent. The houris are described as wearing very sweet-smelling clothes.

Some buildings have been described as being constructed of bricks of gold and silver with mortar of musk, which is used to make perfume.

When outdoors, there will be a smell of musk, which is said to be the most common smell in heaven. Apart from that, there will be the smell of flowers, and the wind will carry a sweet fragrance.

The various foods and drinks in heaven will all have their own delicious aromas. And, mercifully, all foul smells are likely to be missing.

Socializing with Friends and Relatives

People will live with their spouses and tens of thousands of houris and ghilman as servants in their own mansions within their own territories, which could be individual planets. When they want to meet friends and relatives, they'll be able to invite them to their own mansions, travel to visit them in their homes, or meet them at public functions that will be held regularly.

Even though the flow of time will be different in heaven, a calculation based on time as it is on earth will be maintained and according to that, every Friday, there will be public gatherings where people will meet God, and afterwards, they will assemble in a public square, where they will be able to meet people they knew on earth. Those meetings with God will be held more frequently in the upper grades, with the most frequent being twice a day, so presumably the public gatherings will also be more frequent for people in higher levels.

Families will be united before entering heaven. "They will enter perpetual Gardens, along with their righteous ancestors, spouses, and descendants; the angels will go in to them from every gate, 'Peace be with you, because you have remained steadfast. What an excellent reward is this home of yours!'" (13:23-24)

"We unite the believers with their offspring who followed them in faith." (52:21) "They turn to one another and say, 'When we were still with our families [on earth] we used to live in fear—God has been gracious to us and saved us from the torment of intense heat—We used to pray to Him: He is the Good, the Merciful One.'" (52:25-28)

People who didn't get along with one another in this life will be friends in heaven. "And We shall remove any bitterness from their hearts: [they will be like] brothers, sitting on couches, face to face." (15:47)

We have already mentioned that family members, especially spouses, parents, and children will be reunited in heaven, and those earning a place in a lower grade will be upgraded to a higher grade. Since everyone will be the same age in heaven and all generations of people that have ever lived will be together at the same time, it is possible that your great, great grandfather will earn a high grade and pull several generations of descendants, including you, to a higher level. It can work the other way as well. If you earn the highest grade among your relatives, you might pull your grandparents and grandchildren up to a higher position.

People on the same level of heaven will be able to travel to see each other at any time. If people are on different levels, they will still be able to meet. While people on a lower level may not have access to higher levels, people in higher levels will be able to travel to lower levels. Although this information is not one hundred percent confirmed, the reason for this restriction may be in order not to cause people in lower levels to start feeling less blessed.

It is easy to imagine having huge family reunions in heaven. For one thing, your mansion and its grounds will be so large that you'll easily be able to accommodate parties of tens of thousands of people. Also, any reunion in this world is limited to three or four generations, whereas in heaven you'll be able to invite people from a hundred generations if you want. In this world, it is difficult to get many people together because of scheduling and budgetary constraints, but in heaven it will be much easier. The only downside will be that only those people will be able to attend your parties who have made it into heaven.

You will remember everyone you knew in this world, but even if the closest members of your family didn't make it to heaven, you won't feel bad about it because of your altered psyche. There will be a way to get people you love out of hell and into heaven, and we will talk about that in Chapter 11.

You might have a family reunion with thousands of relatives—ancestors you've only heard about, second or third cousins you've never met, or even your great grandchildren who were not yet born when you died.

Since all rancor will have been removed from everyone's hearts, if you didn't get along with someone, you will nevertheless have the best of relations with them in heaven.

Imagine that you're the same age as your grandparents and grandchildren and everyone is physically and spiritually beautiful and you're able to talk with them about old times and laugh and joke about events that happened on earth.

You could have friends over as well, and if you played bridge in this life, you could play it in heaven as well. And you'll have ghilman serving you delicious food and drinks as you sit and chat about old times and maybe even accuse each other of cheating, as you used to do on earth, and laugh about it.

Unlike in this world, there will be no pointless conversations in heaven, nor will anyone tell any lies. "They will hear no idle or sinful talk there, only clean and wholesome speech." (56:25) "There they will hear no vain or lying talk." (78:35) "Where they will hear no idle talk." (88:11)

Music and Entertainment

In this world, we live relatively mundane lives, with the bulk of our time being spent on routine matters such as sleeping, working, eating, cleaning, and other activities. When we have free time, we like to relax by meeting friends, going to movies, visiting art galleries, restaurants, or going on vacations. There's usually a clear distinction between work and leisure activities in this world. In heaven, there will be no work, and every moment will be full of pleasure and entertainment. We will be surrounded by charming people, have thousands of servants at our service and will be living in large mansions of exquisite beauty that we could spend ages exploring. We will therefore not feel any need for other types of entertainment, but every activity that we think of as entertainment in this world will nevertheless be present, such as music, singing, art, parties, sumptuous dinners, etc.

Heaven will be full of music and singing. We will hear the singing of birds, and every time the wind blows, the rustling of tree leaves will sound like music to our ears.

The Prophet said that the houris will sing songs that people will find absolutely fascinating. They will sing about their lives in heaven and also in praise of God. The singing of the angels and the prophets will be even sweeter than the songs of the houris. And the speech of

God, which everyone will be able to hear, will be the most beautiful of all.

The Prophet said: "In Paradise a group of houris will rise and sing in enchanting voices songs that nobody had heard before, saying, 'We are eternal and we are happy, never unfortunate, we have never experienced any sad time.'"

In another hadith, he said, "The houris will sing in heaven, saying, 'We are houris perfected, created for spouses honorable.'"

The Prophet said, "There is a meeting place in paradise for its houris with large eyes. They will raise their voices such as the creatures have never heard, saying, 'We will live forever and we will never die. We live in blessings and will never grieve. We are pleased (with our husbands) and will never be displeased. Happy are they who are for us and we for them.'"[44]

According to the Prophet, "Houris will sing for their own husbands, songs that are so marvelous that every hearer will be pleased. They will say, 'We are houris who have not committed a sin.' The women of this world will reply to them saying, 'We are the ones who fasted and you are not, we are ones who prayed but you are not and we are the ones who gave charity but you are not,'" and the women of this world will win the competition with the houris.[45]

The ultimate entertainment in heaven, if it can be called entertainment, will be the weekly meetings with God, during which the angels will sing and prophets will recite the scriptures, and we will hear the speech of God himself. It is said that God will ask the angels to sing, and they will chant the divine names in such a beautiful way that such hymns would have never ever been heard before.[46] We will talk about this meeting with God in the next chapter.

There will be many public receptions, during which sumptuous meals will be laid out on tables and ghilman will serve countless courses of food and drinks. People will be accompanied by their spouses, and there will be great conversations and a lot of joking and laughing, without anyone ever offending anyone else, as everyone will maintain the best of manners in heaven. There will be wine and drinking without any intoxication or inappropriate behavior.

Some people have asked about the point of having wine if it won't make you inebriated. The answer is that wine in heaven will probably have a mild effect, like making people a little bit happier and lowering their reserve, allowing for smoother conversation, but it will not cause drunkenness. Having too many drinks causes people to say things they regret later, makes them unsteady on their feet, have a hangover the next day, and so on. In heaven, people will enjoy the beneficial aspects of wine, while avoiding any negative side effects.

Talking about the laughter of people in heaven, the Qur'an says, "The wicked used to laugh at the believers—they would wink at one another when the believers passed by them, joke about them when they got back to their own people, and say, when they saw them, 'These people are misguided,' though they were not sent to be their keepers—so today the believers are laughing at the disbelievers as they sit on couches, gazing around." (83:29-35)

There are many forms of entertainment that have not been mentioned in any text, but that doesn't mean that those things will not exist. For example, I haven't seen dancing being mentioned anywhere, but I personally believe that the houris and ghilman will perform beautifully choreographed dances with stunningly beautiful singing and music. For some reason, this comes to my mind as one of the most beautiful forms of entertainment in heaven.

Other things that have not been mentioned are things such as theater, art galleries, museums, libraries, or sports. I think that all of these things will be there, but at the time of the Prophet, living in a small town in the middle of the desert fourteen hundred years ago, it would have been hard for people to visualize these things.

What You Will Get in Heaven 211

Everything that we want heaven to have but that has not been mentioned will come under the category of things that, "The eye has not seen, the ear has not heard, and the heart has not imagined." Today we can imagine many things that people in olden times could not, but we still cannot imagine many things that might exist one thousand years into the future, but all these things will be there in heaven, and more.

God promises in the Qur'an, "They will have all that they wish for there, and We have more for them." (50:35) So, everyone will get whatever they ask for, and "more" refers to things that are beyond anything you could even imagine asking for.

Someone asked the Prophet what it means when the Qur'an mentions, "We have more for them," and the Prophet replied that it includes meeting with God, which will be the ultimate experience in heaven.[47] I refer to the "more" that's been promised as "special favor" in the next chapter. The Prophet also mentioned that one day a man would be lying on a couch and a stunningly beautiful houri would come to him and he would ask her who she is and she would reply, "I'm part of the 'more' that you've been promised."[48]

If you wanted a grand museum with all the artifacts from all the museums on earth, you'll get it in the blink of an eye. Then, you could spend years exploring it. If you wanted to look at every painting by Leonardo Da Vinci, it will be possible for you to do so. I can go on describing the endless things you could ask for, but I leave it to your imagination to figure out what it is that you would like.

Here's something I would like: I would like to go back in time in this world and watch events from history as they're happening, such as going back to the time of the prophets and watching prophets Muhammad and Jesus preaching, visiting the courts of past kings and emperors, watching famous battles as they happen—all the things I've read about in history books. We know that everything that has ever happened has been recorded, so it should be possible to watch all those events from the perspective of an invisible spectator standing in the middle of the activity. It would just be a recording we would be watching, so there won't be any possibility of interfering in anything.

Language of Heaven

It is not clear what language will be spoken in heaven. Some people say that it will be Arabic, but that claim is based on weak chains of hadith and therefore doubtful.

It is likely that a totally new language will be the lingua franca. It may be a new language altogether or an advanced version of one of the languages spoken in this world. Everyone will also remember the languages they spoke in this world.

There will be new information programmed into our brains when we arrive in heaven. It was mentioned by the Prophet that everyone would know their way around their mansions when they arrive at their new homes. I believe that a single common language will be programmed into everyone's brain, and as soon as we enter heaven, we will be speaking it as comfortably as if it were our native tongue.

Languages we spoke in this world will also be part of our memories, and we will get the opportunity to use them with our family, relatives, and friends who also spoke the same language.

It is also possible that people will be able to understand every language that is spoken. The Prophet mentioned that in the meeting with God, David will recite the Psalms and Muhammad will recite the Qur'an; therefore, it may be that people will understand the verses as they're being recited in their original tongues.

I like learning new languages, and I believe that if I'm not able to master a language I want to learn in this world, I will be able to do so in heaven. There are maybe half a dozen languages I would like to learn.

8

Meeting God— The Ultimate Experience

"Whoever loves to meet God, God loves to meet him. And whoever hates to meet God, God hates to meet him."
- Prophet Muhammad [1]

All the extraordinary luxuries of heaven described up to now will pale into insignificance compared to the ultimate pleasure we will experience when we meet God face to face.

Someone may well ask why meeting God will be more pleasurable than everything else. The most simple and logical answer is that it will be so because God has designed us in such a way that the maximum happiness we can ever experience will come from being in his own presence.

Let's ask a philosophical question: "Is there a limit to beauty?" In other words, is there something so beautiful out there that there cannot be anything better than that? Even though it is said that beauty is in the eye of the beholder, it is also true that most people generally agree when something is aesthetically pleasing. If we have a competition for the most attractive person in the world and make a selection, will it be possible to find someone even more beautiful than that? Maybe not on earth, but in heaven, there will be beings—humans, angels, ghilman, and houris—much more good-looking than the most beautiful person on earth. That's because everyone in heaven, human or nonhuman, will be better than anyone on earth.

Even among people in heaven, there will be some who will be more beautiful than others. While the least will be better than anyone on earth, people in higher grades will be superior to them, and the ones on the highest level of heaven will be the most superior.

In heaven, therefore, there appears to be no limit to beauty, and people and things will just keep getting infinitely better and more attractive as you go up the grades of heaven. But there will be an ultimate limit and that will be God himself, who will be the most beautiful being of all. When we see him, we will know that God has the maximum beauty that can be attained by anyone or anything in all of existence. That is because God is the one who created beauty, and he has made himself the most beautiful. The Prophet said, "God is beautiful and loves beauty."[2]

A similar question can be asked about feelings of pleasure and happiness. "Is there a limit to how happy we can feel?" And the answer is the same: that in this world, the maximum happiness we can feel will pale into insignificance compared to the happiness of being in heaven, and as we go higher up the levels of heaven, people will be even happier. This is so because if people in various levels will have similar levels of happiness, then there will be no purpose for having higher levels.

So the higher the grade of heaven a person will be in, the happier he will be, and therefore feelings of pleasure and happiness will appear to increase all the way up to infinity. But there will be an upper limit to happiness and that will be attained when we see God. That will be so because God himself has created the experience of happiness, and he has made it such that maximum happiness can only be attained when someone is in his presence.

With the thought that the most beautiful thing we will ever see will be God and the maximum happiness we can ever attain will be experienced when we see him, let's move on to the details of meeting with God, as they have been described in the sayings of the Prophet.

There are many versions of the Prophet's sayings about the meeting with God, some with more details and some with less. I have collected them from various sources and combined them to create one narrative. One of the most profound and detailed descriptions I have found is in an interview of Sheikh Ibrahim Dremali, who has a PhD in Islamic Law from Al-Azhar University in Cairo. This interview is available on YouTube if you would like to watch it yourself.[3]

During that meeting, when God will talk to people publicly, they will always reply in unison because their hearts will be alike and their thinking process will be the same.

Talking about God, the Prophet said, "His veil is the light. If he withdraws it (the veil), the splendor of his countenance would consume his creation as far as his sight reaches."[4] At first, when God will appear to people, his true self will be hidden from view behind a veil of light. Later, he will remove the veil and become visible directly. This is something that is not possible in this world, but will be so in heaven. Because of the new laws of physics in heaven, we will be able to look at God directly without any screen or barrier.

Meeting God—The Ultimate Experience

In heaven, you will be living in your mansion, and it will have a special door through which an angel will enter every Friday[5] and deliver a beautiful little invitation card to you from God that will say, "My servant, I miss you, come and visit me."

As you step outside your mansion, a perfumed wind will blow and cover you with fragrance. You will hasten to a special gathering place in a wide river valley where there will be seating arrangements for vast numbers of people who will be arriving from all parts of heaven. It is said that this meeting place is in Firdaus, which is the highest grade of heaven.

The Throne of God will be visible in the sky, and chairs, like thrones, will be arranged based on the rank of each person and will be marked with their names. Some chairs will be made of light, some of pearls, some of rubies, aquamarine, gold, silver, and so on, and no one will see the seating arrangements of people of higher ranks, and there will be no feelings of being seated lower than anyone else—everyone will feel as though they're the most honored of all.[6]

Though unseen at the moment, God will be directing the angels. He will be telling them, "Oh my angels, they are my servants, the ones I love, my family; honor them, give them food and drinks."

When you arrive at the gathering place, angels will usher you to your seat, and you will sit down waiting for the meeting to start. Your chair will be very comfortable, and you will sit down in a casual way while angels will serve food and drinks.

Once everyone is seated, anticipation will build up as people will wait for the appearance of God. An angel will call, "Oh people of heaven, you have an appointment with God in which he wishes to reward you."

People will reply, "And what is that reward? Has he not already made our faces bright, forgiven us, and entered us into paradise and pushed us away from the fire?"

Suddenly, there will be massive illumination that will encompass all of heaven, as God will appear behind a veil of light. They will raise their heads and will look up and see God himself. He will say, "Oh people of heaven, peace be on you." [7]

People will say, "Oh God! You are peace and from you is peace. Blessed are you, possessor of majesty and honor."

God will laugh and say, "Where are my servants who used to obey me without ever having seen me? This is the day of special favor." This special favor is what is referred to in the Qur'an as God saying, "We have 'more' for them."

So everyone present will respond in one voice, "We are pleased, so be pleased with us."

God will say, "Oh people of heaven, if I were not pleased with you, I would not have made you inhabitants of my heaven. This is the day of special favor, so ask of me."

They will all give the same response, "Show us your face so that we can look at it."

Then God will remove his veil and his real face will become visible, and God will intend them not to be harmed, otherwise they would get burned from the effects of his divine countenance being uncovered. In this world, it is not possible for God to reveal himself without catastrophic damage being caused to the beholder and the surroundings.

Everyone present, including the angels, will see God and will be so stunned by his magnificence that they will say, "Oh God! We did not pay esteem to you as you had the right to be esteemed, and we did not worship you as you deserved to be worshipped."

People will try to get up to bow down to worship God, but they will be prevented from doing so, and God will say to them, "Raise your head, this is not a day of prayer. Instead, it is a day of enjoyment and benevolence."[8] They will be told that they had worshipped God enough on earth, and now the time of worship is over and it is no longer necessary.

People will praise God and be thankful to him with every breath, but formal worship will have been abolished, and bowing down will not be required or allowed. God will tell people that they're his guests, and guests only receive favors and are not expected to do anything in return.[9]

Then God will speak to each person individually, and he will say, "Do you remember the day you did such and such, and will remind a person of some of his bad deeds," to which the person will reply, "Oh Lord, won't you forgive me?"

He will say, "Of course! You have not reached this position of yours (in heaven) except by my forgiveness."[10]

Another narrative has a slightly different version of the meeting, but it could be describing another meeting, since these get-togethers will be held once every week.[11]

God will tell the angels, "They are my servants who prohibited their ears from hearing false talk and forbidden songs and music. Now, I will make them hear the most beautiful songs and music."

God will ask the prophet David to get up and recite the Psalms. When David will begin to recite the Psalms, the birds will recite along with him and the rivers will stop flowing. God will say, "My servants, have you ever heard anything more beautiful than that?"

The people will say, "Oh Lord, by your glory and power, we've never heard anything more beautiful than that."

God will say, "I will make you hear something even more beautiful than that."

Then he will say, "Stand up, Muhammad, and recite to them Surah Taha," which is chapter 20 of the Qur'an.

Then Muhammad will get up and recite Surah Taha and God will say, "My servants, have you ever heard anything more beautiful than that?"

The people will say, "Oh Lord, by your glory and power, we've never heard anything more beautiful than that."

God will say, "I will make you hear and see something even more beautiful than that."

Then God will reveal his face and you will see his real self. He will recite Surah Rehman, which is chapter 55 of the Qur'an. Then he will say, "My servants, have you ever heard anything more beautiful than that?"

The people will say, "Oh Lord, by your glory and power, we've never heard anything more beautiful than that."

God will say, "My servants, be in my heaven, I will never give you a hard time."

According to another narration, God will say, "Oh people of paradise!"

They will reply, "Here I am, oh Lord, at your service."

God will say, "Are you pleased?"

They will say, "Why should we not be pleased, since you have given us what you have not given to anyone of your creation?"

God will say, "I will give you something better than that."

They will reply, "Oh our Lord! And what is better than that?"

God will say, "I will bestow my pleasure and contentment upon you so that I will never be angry with you forever."[12]

Never being angry again will be a special favor from God. Adam and Eve were also in heaven, but there was something they did that made God angry and got them expelled. When God will tell us that he will never be angry with us again, it will mean that there is absolutely nothing we can do in heaven that will displease God, which implies that there will be no chance of ever being expelled again.

During this meeting, some time will be spent during which God will be addressing the gathering publicly, but then, he will turn his attention to each individual and have a one-to-one conversation with them. This is an example of God's omnipresence, the quality of being able to be present everywhere at the same time. To each individual, it will seem as though God were talking to him or her and no one else.

Meeting God—The Ultimate Experience

This will be the experience to surpass every other experience in heaven. You will be looking directly at the face of God, which will be the most beautiful vision you have ever seen, or will ever see. You will be in a state of ecstasy that will surpass any feeling of happiness you will ever have. You will feel that nothing exists but you and God, and you will be talking to him. All your sins will have been forgiven, and God will be pleased with you, so you will have nothing to fear.

God will discuss your entire life with you, moment by moment. You will be able to ask him about the times when you prayed to him, and he will tell you he was there listening to you, and why and how he answered your prayer. Every prayer is answered; it's just that the result is not always what we demand.

You could ask him about the secrets of the universe and ask why he created us in the first place, how many universes there are, and countless other questions that you may have but don't know the answer to.

God will ask you if there is anything else you would like to have, and you will be able to ask him for anything you want. It has been said that people will ask only for things that are valid; their changed psyche and perfect manners in heaven will not allow them to ask for things that they should not be asking for. For example, no one will ask to be upgraded to a higher grade in heaven, because they will be more than satisfied with what they have.

These meetings will be held at least once a week for all of eternity, so each of us could become what we may term "buddies" with God. People of higher grades will meet God more frequently, with the people of the highest rank meeting him twice a day.

Meanwhile, a cloud will come over them and rain down on them perfume with a fragrance the like of which they will never have experienced before. God will say, "Get up and go to the honor that has been prepared for you, and take whatever you desire."

9

Shopping Malls of Heaven

Every Friday after the meeting with God, you will proceed to a nearby marketplace that will be located in a huge city square.[1] As you are walking there, your mind will be engrossed in thoughts of just having seen and talked with God, and these thoughts will linger in your mind and you will continue to derive pleasure from them until the next meeting a week later.

Meanwhile, you will be walking into a city where you will shop for gifts for yourself and your family, and will also get to meet other people from all over heaven, both people you knew in this life and new people with whom you will make friends.

The idea behind the existence of this marketplace is important to appreciate. Having just come from a meeting with God, we will experience the maximum spiritual high that is possible. Since we will have physical bodies, experiencing the fulfillment of all our material desires will also be an integral part of our pleasure of living in heaven, and this market will allow us to indulge in all our materialistic fantasies.

The Prophet said that the places most loved by God are mosques and the places most hated by him are the markets.[2] That applies to this world, where a place of worship represents nearness to God, while in markets, people indulge in worldly affairs and forget about God. But in heaven, there will be no places of worship, and many things that are disapproved of in this world, such as wine, will be freely available.

Materialism in itself is not a bad thing, but only becomes so in this world when it causes us to neglect the remembrance of God or to indulge in sinful actions in order to acquire material benefits. As long as worldly goods are obtained in a legal manner, and the charity that is due on our assets is paid, we are free to enjoy our possessions. God says in the Qur'an, "Say [Prophet], 'Who has forbidden the adornment and the nourishment God has provided for His servants?' Say, 'They are [allowed] for those who believe during the life of this world: they will be theirs alone on the Day of Resurrection.'" (7:32)

Material possessions are freely available to everyone in this world, but in the next life they will only be available to those who go to heaven, and they will be given gifts of exquisite beauty and in great quantities.

At the end of the meeting with God, he will have told us that he has prepared blessings for us to take, as we desire. In heaven, all resource constraints that we experience in this world will have been removed. It will be a majestic display of God's generosity and power and a show of his ability to create things of ingenious design, immense beauty, and infinite quantity and quality. It will be a refutation of those who complain of God's resources being limited.

Imagine a vast city with countless buildings with shops, restaurants, and open public spaces. People will be arriving there in the millions from the meeting with God. The streets will be paved with gold and silver bricks, and the buildings will also be made of alternating bricks of gold and silver and studded with precious gemstones. It will be the most wonderful city you've ever seen, beautiful beyond imagination.

Think of the biggest shopping mall you've ever seen, and then multiply that by a million. The whole city will be a vast shopping center with buildings and shops as far as the eye can see.

Angels will be attending shops[3] where there will be goods on display that, "eyes haven't seen, ears haven't heard, and minds haven't imagined." You will be welcome to take what you like as gifts from God. There will be no limit to what you will be allowed to take, and you will not have to pay for anything.

Since details of the goods on display are scant, we can only speculate about what will be available. Imagine going to a large, modern shopping mall and looking around to see what kinds of goods are being sold there, and then assume that the shopping malls in heaven will have similar goods, but of infinitely better quality. Clothes have been mentioned in the Hadith, and modern shopping malls also mostly consist of clothing stores. There are also likely to be shoes, jewelry, perfumes, furniture, home furnishings, and even automobiles.

What about electronic goods? If we look at some of the electronic gadgets we have today, they would have seemed magical to people even a couple of hundred years ago. A person living fourteen hundred years ago certainly wouldn't have been able to imagine things such as computers, digital cameras, and mobile devices like iPhones. Can you imagine what kind of things will exist one thousand years from now? What will be available in the market in heaven may be a million years more advanced than what we have now, so there will certainly be things available that we cannot even imagine.

You will be able to walk around the market selecting anything you want to your heart's content. Your goods will be shipped off to your mansion, so you won't have to worry about carrying shopping bags.[4]

One of the characteristics of these marketplaces that have been described is that people from various levels will be able to meet each other there.

Clothing

The Prophet said that there will be mannequins displaying beautiful clothes for both men and women. If you like a set of clothes, they will automatically appear on your body for you to try out,[5] and visiting a dressing room will not be necessary. You'll be able to try on as many clothes as you like and take whichever ones you want.

The Qur'an mentions silk as the material that clothes will be made from. "There they will be adorned with bracelets of gold. There they will wear garments of fine silk and brocade." (18:31)

The clothes will be made of silk and brocade inlaid with exquisite gold embroidery. They will not have been manufactured in factories, but will emerge out of the flowers of special trees.[6] In another place, it is said that the clothes will be made from the calyx, which is the outer casing of flowers. To me, it sounds like some kind of advanced technology that will allow garments to be manufactured like this. Calling them trees is just a figure of speech. Angels will then pick the clothes from the "flowers" and put them on display in the shops.

You will select clothes for yourself, and it is likely that you will also take some for your spouse and maybe even for your favorite servants among the houris and ghilman.

Angels will be manning the aisles and taking orders. Once you've selected your clothes, you might keep wearing the ones you like and have the rest shipped to your mansion.

You will have huge rooms in your mansion for keeping clothes, probably many times larger than the biggest homes in this world, so there should be no shortage of space for keeping your newly acquired clothes. With no poor people in heaven, it will not be possible to give old clothes away, unless friends and relatives would like some of them. Clothes in heaven will be as eternal as everything else and will not be subject to being soiled, wrinkled, torn, or worn out.[7] They will remain in perfect condition, so other people in heaven might take some if you want to give them away.

Will there be designer clothes? I don't know for certain, but I can say that the clothes that people in the upper levels of heaven will wear are said to be superior to the ones in the lower levels. So the clothes of higher-ranking inhabitants of heaven could be called designer clothes, just as rich people on earth wear more exclusive brands. There will certainly be a great variety of clothes made from many different materials and many different designs. I think that clothes will be a major topic of discussion in heaven. We may talk about which part of heaven they come from, what materials they're made from, details of their design, and so on.

There is a hadith according to which when two people meet and one of them is wearing clothes of a quality superior to the other, the clothes of the person of lower rank will automatically change to match the clothes of the higher ranking person. This is so that no one ever gets a feeling of being less blessed than anyone else in any way.[8]

All of the clothes will be of the highest quality, but some will be better than others. Heaven will not be a uniform place, but full of variety and will have everything that will make it interesting.

Jewelry

Unlike this world, where jewelry is usually worn only by women, and usually only on special occasions, in heaven, both men and women will wear jewelry all the time; after all, they will always be dressed like kings and queens.

You will have a crown on your head made of gold and inlaid with precious stones such as pearls, emeralds, rubies, sapphires, and diamonds. On your hands, you will have bracelets of gold or silver, and will probably also have necklaces, rings, and other accessories. Therefore, you will require lots of jewelry, and shopping for new items will probably become an important part of your regular shopping expeditions.

Heaven will be full of precious materials; in fact, everything, including buildings, will be made from gold, silver, rubies, emeralds, pearls, diamonds, and anything rare and expensive you can think of. Similarly, the shops will be full of large quantities of jewelry of great quality, variety, and beauty. And whatever you want will be yours.

Perfumes

Perfumes will also be a very important part of your personal grooming regimen in heaven. Everything, including buildings and the air you breathe, will be full of fragrance, and your hair, body, and clothes will always be perfumed.

The Prophet recommended giving perfume as a gift and advised people, "If one of you is offered a scent, let him not refuse it, for it comes from Paradise."[9] The nicest things in this world remind us of heaven, and perfume is one of them.

There will likely be a great variety of perfumes in heaven; some similar to ones in this world, but many that will be totally new to us. With so many fragrances to choose from, hopefully, there will be knowledgeable angels who would ask us a few questions about our personal tastes and then recommend perfumes that we will like.

Imagine the largest department store you can think of and multiply it many times, then imagine it to be full of millions of varieties of exotic scents and perfumes, each one better than anything you have ever smelled before. I can imagine myself spending a lot of time there chatting with the angels and trying out hundreds, if not thousands, of different fragrances. The best part will be that the angels won't get upset if I haven't bought something after trying a few, as would be the case in any store here on earth.

Other Goods

Like everything else, there will probably be infinite designs and colors of shoes on display, and they'll be studded with rubies, diamonds, and other precious stones.

Women are already used to having many different designs of shoes to choose from, while men's shoes, like the rest of men's clothing in this world, are usually very bland. Black and brown shoes make up the bulk of men's footwear, apart from some colorful sports shoes. I hope to find many more designs of shoes for men, which, just like the rest of men's clothing, will also be a lot fancier than what we're used to here.

As with clothes, it is likely that if you see a shoe on display that you like, it will immediately appear on your feet. If you like it, you'll be able to take it, otherwise the one you were previously wearing will appear back on your feet.

There should be other goods on display too, such as furniture, home furnishings, and any other kind of thing you can imagine, as well as many things you cannot imagine. Heaven will be a futuristic environment, not an old-fashioned one, and therefore, everything will be appropriately advanced in design and quality.

Our mansions will be very large and furnished with beautiful furniture. Luxurious couches have been mentioned several times in the Qur'an, but mostly in an outdoor setting, where people will be attending gatherings. "The people of Paradise today are happily occupied—they and their spouses—seated on couches in the shade." (36:55-56) Couches inside mansions have been mentioned in the Hadith. Thrones have also been referred to, which will be elaborately decorated chairs.

There is little or no mention in the Qur'an and Hadith of other items of furniture, such as tables, beds, coffee tables, chests of drawers, etc., but it is easy to imagine that they will be present in those large mansions with thousands of rooms. At the marketplace, furniture should be available for you to redecorate your home. Some of them may be made of solid gold or silver and be decorated with gemstones. It is possible that there will be wood furniture as well, but most of the furniture is likely to be made from precious materials.

Tableware has been mentioned in the Qur'an to be made from gold or silver. "They will be served with silver plates and gleaming silver goblets according to their fancy." (76:15-16) Dishes will be made from pure silver, and cups will also be made of silver that will be transparent like crystal. In the upper levels of heaven, crockery will be made from gold.

I would like to believe that there will also be decorative pieces, such as statues, vases, lamps, and anything else we can imagine.

Vehicles

I'm a bit of a car enthusiast, and I love to imagine what heaven has in store for us as means of transportation. Everyone needs some form of transportation, although some people in this world also enjoy automobiles as a hobby. That will also be the case in heaven, because it will be so much larger than earth, and travel distances will be vast, so everyone will need something to ride on. Even getting around our own homes might require some form of vehicle unless we want to spend days walking around the huge houses.

As far as I know, people in heaven will not be able to fly like Superman, and there will be physical limitations to what people would be able to do.

Will it be possible that in heaven people will teleport to various locations? That would mean dematerializing in one location and materializing in another, like being beamed to various locations in Star Trek. I think that that may be possible, although it's not been confirmed in any text that I know of. What I have found mentioned are winged horses made from red rubies, or pearls, that will transport people to their destinations.[10] That implies that physical transportation devices will exist, although it doesn't preclude teleportation. Therefore, I like to imagine that the winged horses made from red rubies will actually be advanced flying machines made from precious materials like everything else in heaven.

Just as we love cars today, in the past, people used to love horses and used to own and breed them for pleasure. Even the Qur'an mentions this. "The love of desirable things is made alluring for men—women, children, gold and silver treasures piled up high, horses with fine markings, livestock, and farmland—these may be the joys of this life, but God has the best place to return to." (3:14) God is saying that we may love the luxuries of this world, but he has much better things for us in the next world. That will include substitutes for horses, which today are cars; in the future they might be spaceships, and we can only guess what they will be in heaven.

If people could afford them in this world, almost everyone would be driving exotic cars, such as Rolls Royces, Ferraris, and Lamborghinis, or even flying private jets. I believe that heaven will have futuristic flying machines that will leave Lamborghinis or Learjets in the dust, and each one of us will have them. That means that we will be able to acquire new ones, and therefore they should be available in the shopping malls of heaven.

You might be able to go to the "auto dealerships" in the marketplace and check out the latest and greatest models on display. Instead of being like car dealerships, these could be more like vast hangars where companies such as Boeing and Airbus might display their jetliners. Some could be small personal devices, while there would be large spaceships for interplanetary travel.

My own imagination stops at the point of thinking of spaceships, as we see in sci-fi movies, but you can carry on imagining where I leave off. We could walk around checking them out and order the ones we like to be delivered to our homes.

Public Square and Meeting People

We have been told that at this market square, we will meet people from all over heaven. Many will be those we knew in this world, and we will also have the opportunity to become acquainted with people we have never met before. Imagine that everyone who has ever lived will be present at the same time in heaven, and we will be able to meet all those famous people we've always heard about, including prophets, kings, explorers, inventors, and other great personalities, assuming they'll be in heaven, of course.

After you will have finished shopping, you'll go out and walk around the public square, mingling in the crowds. You should have communication links with other people, like we have smart phones, and be able to coordinate with others on where to meet. At previous visits to the marketplace, you would have gotten in touch with great numbers of family members, past and future relatives, as well as friends, and you will also have made lots of new friends, so your contact list may run into the thousands. Depending on whom you want to link up with that day, you could send them a message to meet you, or maybe you will already have an appointment that you made a million years ago with a personality who is in great demand.

Everyone in heaven will be generous and friendly, with arrogance being one of the things having been banished, so famous personalities whom you contact will be happy to meet you and make an appointment to see you, depending on their availability. Since you will have eternity ahead of you, your appointment calendar could stretch into hundreds of thousands of years. You will have the time to meet every single person you want to meet, not just once, but many times.

If you meet a person of higher rank than you, and he's wearing nicer clothes than you are, your own clothes will change to match his for finery. This is so that no one feels less honored than anyone else.

Restaurants and Bars

The activity in heaven that's been mentioned the most in the Qur'an is attending sumptuous receptions while being served food and drinks by ghilman, and I believe that this marketplace will contain countless restaurants with both indoor and outdoor seating, serving great food.

In this world, shopping malls usually have food courts, and when shoppers get fatigued from walking around, they end up crowding the fast-food restaurants. In heaven, we will not get tired or hungry, but we will eat and drink for pleasure, although our bodies may require a minimal amount of nourishment.

We will go to the restaurants to try out the different foods available and to socialize with the many friends and relatives we will meet at the gathering. If we can have such a great variety of restaurants in this world, we should have many more types of restaurants in that place, with foods from different parts of heaven having different cooking styles and using exotic ingredients. There should be beautiful décor and impeccable service. The best part will be the great company we will find ourselves in and the interesting conversations we will have with them.

Imagine that today in heaven you have an appointment to meet one of the great prophets, maybe Jesus or Muhammad. You would meet him and suggest a restaurant that you like, and just the two of you will walk over and be greeted by angels or ghilman and be seated at your table. No one is likely to disturb your conversation because people will have impeccable manners and will know when to leave you alone.

You would be seated at your table with your favorite prophet, and you'll be able to discuss their teachings and compare them with the knowledge you had about them.

I can say with confidence that any prophet you meet will tell you that their teachings were the same: "Believe in one God and worship him and do good deeds in your life, and you'll go to heaven." You would have followed that basic advice, which is why you would be there.

Ghilman will come to serve you, and you could order many different dishes and be able to eat all of them without a problem. Maybe you'll try to prolong the occasion if you've got some great personality with you that day and order a hundred-course dinner, with each course being a full meal. One lesser-known hadith describes some people having three-hundred course dinners at home, so a hundred may not be considered excessive.

You'll have wine with your meal, but maybe after dinner you'll suggest going to a bar and having a few drinks. To some Muslims with sensitive personalities, it may sound incredible to hear of going to a bar with a prophet for drinks, but wine has been mentioned multiple times in the Qur'an. "A drink will be passed round among them from a flowing spring: white, delicious to those who taste it, causing no headiness or intoxication." (37:45) As already explained in Chapter 7, alcohol will be present, but it will not cause drunkenness or lead to inappropriate behavior.

If there will be restaurants in heaven, then there's no reason why there cannot be bars dedicated to serving countless types of wines and other drinks from all over heaven.

For what it's worth, twice I've seen in dreams that I'm standing at a bar very much like the ones we have in this world, where the barmen are angels serving drinks. Before that, I had no concept of there being bars in heaven, and the dreams seemed a bit incongruent because of the Islamic prohibition on alcohol, but in light of the statements in the Qur'an and Hadith mentioning wine in heaven, I've interpreted the dreams to mean that there actually might be bars serving alcohol in heaven.

You could go to one of those bars with your honorable companion and continue your conversation. You could try different drinks and, as with eating, you would be able to drink enormous amounts of beverages without feeling full, getting intoxicated, or having to go to the washroom.

Finally, you'll be ready to say goodbye to your companion. Before parting, you might schedule another appointment with him for one thousand years later. Then, you'll step outside to see what else you can find.

Museums, Art Galleries, and Libraries

Heaven will be an advanced version of this world and will have everything good that we have, and more. Therefore, it is fair to say that there will be all those things we enjoy, even if they're not mentioned in religious texts.

For one thing, the writings that have come down to us are only fragments of what Moses, Jesus, Muhammad, or any other prophet actually said. Secondly, in those times, the prophets could only have mentioned things that people would have been interested in or understood. And finally, even the prophets will have been given only partial knowledge of what's in store in heaven, and not all of it. For example, would Moses and his people have been interested if God had told them about art galleries in heaven? They were living in the middle of a desert, with matters of daily survival to worry about. Just the promise of receiving food every day would have seemed like heaven to them.

It's important to follow the general principle of what heaven will be like, according to which everything good in this earth will be there and a whole lot more that is beyond our imagination.

Following that principle, we should be able to say that there will be museums, libraries, art galleries, theaters, lecture halls, educational facilities, and so on. They'll be located in the city square that we're presently discussing. This place will be like a city center similar to a downtown area in a modern metropolitan city, where people live in the suburbs and travel to the downtown area, where all the major buildings and shopping centers are located.

In heaven, the suburbs will be countless planets scattered about widely, but on regular occasions, we will be traveling to a central location to meet God and then go to the marketplace to shop and mingle with people. It is likely that all the facilities related to arts, culture, and education will be located here in the city center.

We could go to a museum of ancient civilizations and find original artifacts from Egypt, Babylon, Greece, Rome, and so on. There could be an art gallery with medieval European paintings. All of these will be far better equipped than the museums of today. Maybe the latest gadgets we have today will be on display as ancient relics in a museum in heaven; things like iPhones and Samsung Galaxies. We could laugh at how primitive these things were compared to what we will have then.

I firmly believe that we will also get the opportunity to further our education. We will not be born in heaven with knowledge of everything, and our level of education will be pretty much the same as we had when we left the earth; therefore, we will be able to benefit from learning new things, such as a new language or skill, or to take some courses on the new physics and biology of heaven.

Home Again

Every time you return home from your meeting with God and visiting the marketplace, you will tell your spouse that you've just come back from a meeting with God. Your spouse will say, "By God, you look even more beautiful than when you left," and you'll say the same to her or him. The houri or ghilman spouses are referred to here, as they will be staying at home and not going on the trip to meet God.

10

What Heaven Will Not Have

It's easy to start imagining that everything we have in this world will also be available in heaven, but that is far from the truth. In reality, many things we're familiar with will not exist in heaven. I'll try to list some of them.

We already know that our bodies will be different. That will eliminate everything associated with toilet functions, such as restrooms and all the paraphernalia we need, including bathroom tissue, and so on. Since there will be no disease, there will be no medicines, doctors, clinics, hospitals, or any kind of medical facilities.

Our psyche will be different, and negative thoughts will not exist. That will eliminate things such as crude jokes, backbiting, arrogance, or anything that results in people being hurt in any way. It also removes mental health clinics or anything related to aberrant behavior.

There will be no courts, judges, lawyers, police, or jails. People who are criminals in this world will be locked away securely in hell, and those who will be let out and brought into heaven will behave like angels, and therefore, there will be no need for any law enforcement.

There is no concept of working for a living in heaven. We will be guests of God, and he will not allow us to work to earn our keep. Everything we need will be provided free of charge, and we wouldn't be expected to pay for anything. There will be thousands of servants, and we won't even be required to cook our meals or clean the house. If we want to pursue creative activities such as education, art, handicrafts, etc., we will likely have those things to keep us amused, but it won't be for the purpose of earning money.

Money itself will not exist. Everything will be complimentary, and when we arrive in heaven, we will start out with having more possessions than we will ever need, but we'll be free to acquire more things, and they'll all be available as gifts from God.

With no earnings, and money not even existing, obviously there will be no taxes and no government to regulate our activities. Each person will know the rules of heaven and will follow them automatically. There will be no intrusions into other people's rights, and therefore, there will be no need for law enforcement or government buildings. There may be angels to organize affairs, and they're more likely to be available to serve us rather than behave like haughty government officials. We will be able to ask them to organize something for us, like a reception, and they'll do it diligently.

There will be no factories in heaven. Some advanced automated processes will manufacture everything we require, and the need for pollution-emitting factories, mines, and other manufacturing facilities will have been eliminated. We've already mentioned that clothes will come out of something that will look like trees. Houses and buildings will either be built by angels or materialize instantaneously. It's hard to imagine what the construction process will be like, but it will be something that we'll be able to understand once we're there.

There will be no agriculture. The Prophet confirmed this piece of information when he narrated a story: "One of the inhabitants of paradise will ask God to allow him to cultivate the land. God will ask him, 'Are you not living in the pleasures you like?' He will say, 'Yes, but I like to cultivate the land.'" The Prophet added, "When the man will sow the seeds the plants will grow up and get ripe, ready for reaping and so on till they will be as huge as mountains within a wink. God will then say to him, 'Oh son of Adam! Take, here you are, gather the yield; nothing satisfies you.'"[1]

The biology of heaven will be such that a seed that will be planted will grow and yield its crop in an instant. Fruits that are picked from a tree will be replaced immediately. Birds that are eaten will reassemble and fly away. You will not need to plant a field and wait for a season for it to mature because heaven will run on its own laws and not the laws of nature that apply in this world.

Even things like soil and mud will not be there. The soil in heaven will be saffron and musk and not the organic soil we have here. The pebbles on the ground will be pearls, rubies, and emeralds.

There will be no dairy farming, as we've been told in the Qur'an that milk will flow like a river, and the Prophet told us that there will be an ocean in heaven with milk that will feed the river.

There will be no vineyards in heaven, as we've been told that wine will also flow like a river fed from an ocean.

There will be no childbirth in heaven, as human females and houris will not even possess body parts needed for giving birth. What we have been told is that if someone wants a child, they'll be able to have one, and it will be conceived, born, and grow to the required age in a few minutes, just as plants will grow instantly.[2] This kind of childbirth will be an exception and may be requested only rarely.

With no children being born, there will be no schools and teachers. But I believe that there will be education facilities for adults, so that we can improve ourselves.

When we go to a market in this world, the vast majority of items for sale consists of cheap, low-quality goods, and thankfully those will be missing as well. Everything in heaven will be of high quality and made from precious materials, so we'll be saved from the junk that is piled high and sold cheap in stores.

It is obvious, but I'll mention it anyway, that there will be no wars and killing; therefore, there will be no soldiers, weaponry, armament factories, or research facilities inventing new and more "efficient" ways of killing people.

None of the reasons for which humans fight will be present. There will be no lack of resources. There will be no ethnic groups, based on the information available. There will be a common language and a common religion; a religion of belief in God and being thankful to him and praising him.

There will be no places of worship, since formal worship will have been abolished. People will praise God with each breath in thankfulness for what he will have given them, but there will be no formal religions or temples. The weekly meetings with God will be the substitute for prayers.

The only types of communities existing on the Day of Resurrection will be based on which prophet people followed. Followers of each prophet will group together as they do on earth, but once in heaven, everyone will mix with each other and be like brothers and sisters.

There will be no sun, and light will come from the Throne of God located in the center of heaven. There will be no night, only perpetual daylight.[3]

There will be no hot summers or cold winters, and the weather will change very little and will remain in an optimum condition.

There will be no pollution or foul smells. Garbage and sewerage will be absent. I think that if you left some food on your plate, it will just dissipate into the air or something of that nature. We've been told that a bird that you've just eaten will reassemble and fly away, and the food you eat will be emitted as sweat and evaporate into the air. Since everything is made from atoms, it is possible that all waste that is produced will break down into atoms and just evaporate into the air, and then those atoms will be extracted from the air and recycled to produce something else. So the air itself may be the medium for recycling waste.

Also, I think that harmful substances will not exist. For example, in this world there are plants and trees that produce poisons and other harmful substances; these will not exist in heaven. If you roll around in the grass, you won't end up with bug bites or rashes.

Some animals have been mentioned, but it is not clear if there will be jungles full of wild animals such as tigers, elephants, crocodiles, and such. I believe that since the biological environment in heaven will be so different from earth, these animals will not exist in a wild state, but will be available if someone wants them. If you want a pet tiger, there's a good chance that you'll be able to have one, but I don't believe that tigers will exist in the wild.

Human behaviors that were considered sinful in the past, but which seem to be gaining acceptance lately, such as homosexuality, will not exist in heaven. Even in this world, homosexuality is considered an aberration and is thought to be the result of some biological condition or is a learned social behavior. In heaven, we will all have perfect bodies, whether male or female, and there will be no chance of some physical or psychological condition existing that results in people being attracted to members of the same sex. In heaven, every person will be married to members of the opposite sex, and they'll be extremely happy with that state of affairs. Even if someone is attracted to members of the same sex here on earth, they will find that they've become fully heterosexual in heaven. Any males dreaming of the ghilman will find that they're only attracted to their female spouses in heaven.

Even the wine in heaven will be free of intoxication, so we can eliminate any thoughts of recreational drugs being available. All mind-altering substances are forbidden in this world, and they will not be present in heaven.

One characteristic of this world is that people of lesser means, or lower status, serve others. In the past there were slaves, while today we have maids, servants,, and many other categories of people serving others, such as waiters, cleaners, junior staff, and such. In heaven, each person will be like a king or queen, and no human will serve another. That job will belong to the houris and ghilman.

Boredom

One of the objections some people have raised about living forever in heaven is that they think they will get bored. Let's analyze why people get bored.

One reason could be because of a lack of resources. If you're stuck at home with nothing to do, then you can get bored, but if you had unlimited money, you could just get up and go on a vacation to a beautiful place. Another reason could be because of a lack of friends. If you had a large number of friends, you could visit them or have a party at your house and invite them over.

In heaven, you'll be living a life even better than that of a multi-billionaire, so you won't suffer from any lack of resources or friends. Even if you're very young now, in heaven you'll be an adult and you'll be married and always have company, so there's no chance of ever feeling lonely. You'll be able to have parties at your house or visit other people. You'll have the weekly trip to meet God and then visit the market square, where you'll be able to meet people you know and also make new friends. Everyone will be friendly, so making new friends will be a lot easier than in this world.

There may be an infinite number of interesting events going on all over heaven: parties, movies, restaurants, theaters, concerts, sports, and so on, on a much larger scale than on earth. So, deciding what to do and what not to do may be the main dilemma; it won't be a question of having nothing to do.

The point is that you'll be enjoying every moment of life in heaven, so there will be no possibility of getting tired of it all. If you're having fun, you do not get bored.

Frankly, I find it hard to understand that kind of thinking, maybe because even in this life I keep myself busy, but in heaven, there will be such an endless variety of things to do that I can't imagine ever getting bored. There must be thousands of books I would like to read and thousands of movies I would like to watch. There will be millions of people to meet, planets to explore, and new skills to learn. I can go on and on imagining all the things I would do if I had endless time and wealth to do them; therefore, I'm quite comfortable with the idea of perpetual life.

Boredom and monotony are things that will definitely be missing in heaven.

Sadness

There are so many things in this world that make people sad and miserable, and thankfully, no one will ever be unhappy again once they enter heaven. For one thing, our changed psyche will not allow us to be sad, and in addition, all those external things that cause unhappiness will be missing.

Our changed psyches will eliminate all negative thoughts, so even though we will retain memories of everything, good and bad, that happened to us in this world, it will no longer bother us. Even if we find that some of our loved ones didn't make it into heaven, this won't make us sad or depressed. We will likely understand why God made the decisions he did, and accept them as being fair and reasonable.

All the thousands of other things that cause us physical or mental agony will be missing as well, such as lack of money, stress about paying bills, poor health, and so on.

What Heaven Will Not Have   259

People will have impeccable behavior, so no one is going to laugh or joke about you, behave rudely or insult you. Everyone will be beautiful and healthy, so there will be no reason for any unhappiness about your looks or poor health. There won't be any risk of accidents, injuries, or death for yourself or loved ones. The list of negative things that happen in this world is endless, and none of these will exist in heaven.

We will be devoid of negative thinking within our own minds, and external factors that cause anxiety and sadness will also be missing.

II

How to Go to Heaven

"Paradise is surrounded by hardships, and Hell is surrounded by temptations."

– Prophet Muhammad[1]

If you've read so far, I hope that your appetite has been whetted for wanting to go to heaven. The actions required to get there are hard, but not as difficult as the magnificent reward you will receive, which will be totally out of proportion to anything you can do to earn it. Although the path to heaven is relatively straightforward, making an effort is nevertheless necessary to get there. Unfortunately, most people will not do even what little is required, and we've been told that only a minority of humans will enter paradise.

In this chapter, I will tell you what you need to do to get into heaven from the Islamic point of view. The Qur'an and Hadith have made it very clear what those requirements are, although with the caveat that no one can enter heaven as a right, and ultimately everyone who will be admitted to heaven will enter it because of the mercy of God and his forgiveness of their sins. The Prophet said that even he will only go to heaven because of God's forgiveness.[2]

The Qur'an tells us that on the Day of Judgment, people will be divided into three groups. The first group will consist of those people who were the foremost in closeness to God, who will go to the two upper levels of heaven. The second group will consist of those people who were good and will go to the two lower levels of heaven. The third group will be people who will go to hell, and these will be the majority of people.

The people who will go to hell can be subdivided into two groups. One group will consist of those who will be punished in hell for a while and will then be transferred to heaven. The other group will be those unfortunate people who will go to hell and never get out.

That gives us four groups in total: 1) Best people who will go to the upper levels of heaven, 2) Good people who will go to the lower levels of heaven, 3) People who will be punished in hell but will be moved to heaven, and 4) Those who will remain in hell forever.

Our aim should be to be included in Group 1, but even being included in Group 2 will be okay, as the lower levels of heaven will also be better than anything we can imagine. In a worst-case scenario, even if we could only manage to get into Group 3 and would end up in hell for a while, it will be infinitely better than being condemned to Group 4, which will mean being damned eternally. Even spending a billion years in hell and then being transferred to heaven is better than spending an infinity in hell, since infinity is much longer than a billion years, even longer than a billion times a billion years.

As mentioned in Chapter 4, the Qur'an tells us that many people from the days of old will go to the upper two levels of heaven and few from latter times, while many from both old and latter times will enter the lower two levels of heaven. Since we're now living in latter times, this means that there is a much greater chance of people from today being able to qualify for the lower levels of heaven than for the upper levels, although the best among us can still manage to get into the upper levels.

Both levels of heaven are subdivided into numerous grades, a hundred or more, and whatever good we do raises our grade; therefore, even if we're going to the lower level of heaven, we could still try to qualify for a higher grade in the lower level.

The information I will give you here may be enough to get you into Group 2—going to the lower levels of heaven. To get to the higher levels requires a lot more effort than I can explain in one chapter. Maybe that's a topic for another book, although there may be many books already available on that subject that you could obtain and do your own research.

I would like to remind readers of something I said in Chapter 1 about why God created us:

God created us to worship him.

And this is our purpose in life from our own point of view:

The purpose of life is to go to heaven.

God tells us repeatedly in the Qur'an that the supreme triumph for man is to go to heaven; therefore, if we achieve that, then we would have achieved the objective of life.

Even if someone managed to become a billionaire in this world, he would still not live more than a hundred years or so, and then, he would die like everyone else. Let us suppose that he totally neglected God's commands and lived a life of luxury and hedonism, but after death he ended up in hell. Would it be worth it? He would have exchanged one hundred years of fun for billions of years of misery. Wouldn't he be considered a loser?

Conversely, if someone lived a short, miserable life in this world, living in poverty and want, but when he dies, he ends up in heaven, where he will spend billions of years living like a king. Wouldn't he be considered a winner?

If someone came to you and gave you the choice of living like a billionaire and going to hell or living a short, miserable life and going to heaven, which one would you choose?

The answer to that would depend on whether you believe in God and the afterlife or not. The majority of people in this world would probably opt to live like billionaires and not place too much value on heaven. Most people are concerned with the here and now. They want instant gratification and don't have a firm-enough belief to worry about the hereafter. Only those people whose belief in God and the afterlife is strong will want to sacrifice something in this life in order to go to heaven. Even though heaven is open to everyone, the majority of people will refuse to go there.

The choice between being a billionaire or living in poverty is an extreme example that I've given. In reality, most people who don't believe in God do not become billionaires, nor do all believers live in poverty. In fact, many believers live better lives than many non-believers; therefore, in reality you don't really have to sacrifice much in life to be included among those destined for heaven.

The Prophet said, "All my followers will enter paradise except those who refuse." They said, "Oh God's Apostle! Who will refuse?" He said, "Whoever obeys me will enter paradise, and whoever disobeys me is the one who refuses to enter it."[3]

One day the Prophet met his companions and said: "I saw in a dream that Gabriel stood at the side of my head and Michael by my feet. One of them said to the other, 'Coin for him a parable.' The other said, 'Listen (Muhammad). May your ears listen always. Comprehend. May your heart grasp always. The parable of you and of your community is like a king who takes a house and builds a home. He places there a dining mat and sends a man to invite people to food. There are some who accept his invitation and some who reject him. So, God is the king. The house is Islam and the home is paradise, and you, oh Muhammad, are the messenger. He who answers you, joins Islam and he who joins Islam, enters paradise and he who enters paradise, eats that which is in it.'"[4]

In this book, I don't want to get into a debate about whether there are many paths to heaven apart from Islam. The two main religions that teach belief in God and the afterlife are Christianity and Islam, both of which spring from the same root. I'm going to present the Islamic point of view and also mention Christianity briefly. It will be for you to come to your own conclusion. Since this book is based on Islamic teachings, I will assume you're a Muslim, since the path to heaven, from the Islamic perspective, lies in following the teachings of Islam.

Personally, I would be happy if every single human went to heaven, but the reality is that God is the creator of all existence and has his own purpose for creating us and will do what he pleases, not what we want. An important part of belief is to accept the will of God and submit to it—not that we have much choice in the matter because what he wants will be done, whether we like it or not. God says that he is just and will deal with everyone fairly and with justice. "These are God's revelations: We recite them to you [Prophet] with the Truth. God does not will injustice for His creatures." (3:108)

Those who may feel disgruntled about the fact that not everyone will make it to heaven are not capable of comprehending the wisdom behind God's justice, since our intelligence is very limited compared to the infinite intelligence of God. He says in the Qur'an, "He does not wrong anyone by as much as the weight of a speck of dust: He doubles any good deed and gives a tremendous reward of His own." (4:40)

God maintains the prerogative to punish whomever he wills and forgive anyone he wants. Ultimately, we're trying to earn his forgiveness, but to do so we are required to submit to his will and obey his orders.

Minimum Requirement—Belief in One God

Every person who has faith in his heart so much as the weight of an atom will be taken out of Hell

– Prophet Muhammad[5]

The most basic and minimum requirement without which no one will enter heaven is to believe in God and to worship him only. Anyone who worships any being other than God is not going to enter heaven; it's as simple as that. God says in the Qur'an, "God does not forgive the worship of others beside Him—though He does forgive whoever He will for lesser sins—for whoever does this has gone far, far astray." (4:116)

One of the little acknowledged secrets is the saying of the Prophet who, after a meeting with Gabriel, said, "It was Gabriel who met me by the side of the stony ground and said, 'Give glad tidings to your community that he who died without associating anyone with God would go to paradise.'"[6]

If you believe in God and never associate any other being with him, then you will go to heaven, even if you do not have many good deeds to your credit, although you might have to do a stint in hell, but the point is that you will go to heaven sooner or later. This one little act of believing in one and only one God will earn you a place in heaven, and this is the absolute minimum that you can do to go there.

According to another hadith, the Prophet said, "If anyone testifies that none has the right to be worshipped but God alone who has no partners, and that Muhammad is his slave and his apostle, and that Jesus is God's slave and his apostle and his word which he bestowed on Mary and a spirit created by him, and that heaven is true, and hell is true, God will admit him into paradise with the deeds which he had done even if those deeds were few. Such a person can enter paradise through any of its eight gates he likes."[7]

According to this hadith, a person who says the above might even avoid hell completely, since the hadith appears to be referring to the Day of Judgment, when people will be entering heaven through one of the eight gates. Here, one of the requirements is to accept Jesus as God's slave and apostle.

If someone is not even willing to believe in God, they have no chance of ever entering heaven. "God will admit those who believe and do good deeds to Gardens graced with flowing streams; the disbelievers may take their fill of pleasure in this world, and eat as cattle do, but the Fire will be their home." (47:12)

If you believe in God, but have done bad deeds all your life, then you could end up in Group 3; those who will go to hell for a while, but will then be admitted to heaven.

But we don't want to go to hell, even for a short time. There is a prayer in the Qur'an, "Our Lord, give us good in this world and in the Hereafter, and protect us from the torment of the Fire." (2:201) What this verse of the Qur'an is suggesting is that we pray for being admitted to heaven without ever suffering any punishment at all.

On the Day of Judgment, many people will be put in hell because of their bad deeds, but some of them will be taken out because of their belief in God. The Prophet said, "Whoever said 'None has the right to be worshipped but God' and has in his heart faith equal to the weight of a barley grain will be taken out of hell. And whoever said, 'None has the right to be worshipped but God' and has in his heart faith equal to the weight of a wheat grain will be taken out of hell. And whoever said, 'None has the right to be worshipped but God' and has in his heart faith equal to the weight of an atom will be taken out of hell."[8]

In another place, the Qur'an says, "Every soul will taste death and you will be paid in full only on the Day of Resurrection. Whoever is kept away from the Fire and admitted to the Garden will have triumphed. The present world is only an illusory pleasure." (3:185) The person who is admitted to heaven directly and avoids hell completely will have triumphed.

Believing in God and not worshipping anything or anyone else will get you into heaven at some point in time, but if, despite believing in him, you've never worshipped God or done any good deeds, then you may suffer hell for a while before entering heaven, and that's something that needs to be avoided at all cost. Although we have not gone into the details of hell in this book, I can assure you that it's a very horrific place, and you don't want to go there even for a minute.

In order to have a good chance of entering heaven without ever suffering hell, you will have to do more than just believe in God; you will need to fulfill your obligations to both God and mankind. We will discuss what you need to do in the next sections.

Relationship with God

If you have crossed the first hurdle and believe in God, then you need to establish the correct relationship with him. God knows you better than you know yourself, down to the inner core of your being. "We created man—We know what his soul whispers to him: We are closer to him than his jugular vein." (50:16)

Whatever you're thinking or doing, it is being recorded, and God is aware of your activities. "In whatever matter you [Prophet] may be engaged and whatever part of the Qur'an you are reciting, whatever work you [people] are doing, We witness you when you are engaged in it. Not even the weight of a speck of dust in the earth or sky escapes your Lord, nor anything lesser or greater: it is all written in a clear record." (10:61)

Building an ever-closer relationship with God is how you can rise in rank from the lowest grade of heaven to the highest. You start by believing in him and fulfilling the obligations that he's asked you to fulfill and avoiding those things that he has forbidden. Then you rise in rank by loving God and subordinating your own will to his to the point where you're in total submission to God's will. The word "Islam" means *to submit*, and a Muslim is one who submits to the will of God.

Asking for Forgiveness

"Say, '[God says], My servants who have harmed yourselves by your own excess, do not despair of God's mercy. God forgives all sins: He is truly the Most Forgiving, the Most Merciful.'" (39:53)

All our good and bad deeds are being recorded, and with time we accumulate a whole lot of negative points. This record will be presented to you on the Day of Judgment. We will discuss the point system later in this chapter. To begin a fresh relationship with God, you need to "reboot" the current status of your standing with God and begin with a clean sheet with zero negative points to your credit. You do this by asking for forgiveness for all your past sins.

God told Prophet Muhammad, "Oh son of Adam, so long as you call upon me and ask of me, I shall forgive you for what you have done, and I shall not mind. Oh son of Adam, were your sins to reach the clouds of the sky and were you then to ask forgiveness of me, I would forgive you. Oh son of Adam, were you to come to me with sins nearly as great as the earth and were you then to face me, ascribing no partner to me, I would bring you forgiveness nearly as great as it."[9]

When you ask God for forgiveness, all your past sins are written off, and you start with a clean sheet, as clean as that of a newborn baby. The doors of forgiveness are kept open right up until the moment of death, at which point they're closed, and you will face God on the Day of Judgment with whatever sins you have accumulated. "It is not true repentance when people continue to do evil until death confronts them and then say, 'Now I repent,' nor when they die defiant: We have prepared a painful torment for these." (4:18) The Prophet said that he asks God for forgiveness over seventy times a day.[10]

One of the conditions of asking for forgiveness is that you actually intend to stop committing those sins for which you are asking for forgiveness.

Once you've asked for forgiveness, you can start building up positive points by fulfilling religious obligations and avoiding forbidden things. Then you can rise in status by going beyond the basic requirements and saying extra prayers and worshipping God more than the minimum requirement, giving more in charity, doing good deeds, struggling for God's cause, and increasingly submitting your own will to God's.

Being Grateful

Submitting totally to God's will means loving him unconditionally, obeying him without hesitation (as angels do), accepting his commands without question, always being grateful to him, irrespective of what happens to you—good or bad, always being aware that he's watching you, and totally avoiding whatever he has forbidden.

Being grateful to God for everything he has given us is a very important part of our relationship with him. Conversely, being ungrateful for his blessings is a grievous sin. We need to be thanking him all the time. According to the Qur'an, "It has already been revealed to you [Prophet] and to those before you: 'If you ascribe any partner to God, all your work will come to nothing: you will be one of the losers. No! Worship God alone and be one of those who are grateful to Him.'" (39:65-66)

Fulfilling Religious Obligations

If you do the things you're required to do and avoid forbidden things, then God will love you. The Prophet said, "If God loves a servant, he calls Gabriel and says: 'I love so-and-so, therefore love him.' So Gabriel loves him. Then Gabriel calls out in heaven, saying: 'God loves so-and-so, therefore love him.' And the inhabitants of heaven love him. Then acceptance is established for him on earth."[11] If God loves someone, then people in this world also start loving him.

God said to the Prophet, "I am as my servant thinks I am. I am with him when he makes mention of me. If he makes mention of me to himself, I make mention of him to myself; and if he makes mention of me in an assembly, I make mention of him in an assembly better than it. And if he draws near to me an arm's length, I draw near to him a fathom's length. And if he walks towards Me, I rush towards him."[12]

God told the Prophet, "Whosoever shows enmity to someone devoted to me, I shall be at war with him. My servant draws not near to me with anything more loved by me than the religious duties I have enjoined upon him, and my servant continues to draw near to me with extra works so that I shall love him. When I love him, I am his hearing with which he hears, his seeing with which he sees, his hand with which he strikes, and his foot with which he walks. Were he to ask something of me, I would surely give it to him, and were he to ask me for refuge, I would surely grant him it. I do not hesitate about anything as much as I hesitate about seizing the soul of my faithful servant: he hates death and I hate hurting him."[13]

This sentence—"When I love him, I am his hearing with which he hears, his seeing with which he sees, his hand with which he strikes, and his foot with which he walks," means that a person can get so much in sync with God's will that his thinking and actions are exactly the same as God's. This is a very high level of spiritual advancement.

Beliefs

As a Muslim, there are five things you need to believe in: God, angels, scriptures, prophets, and the Day of Judgment. "You who believe, believe in God, and His Messenger and in the Scripture He sent down to His Messenger, as well as what he sent down before. Anyone who does not believe in God, His angels, His Scriptures, His messengers, and the Last Day has gone far, far astray." (4:136)

The first and foremost doctrine is faith in the absolute unity of God. "Say, He is God the One, God the eternal. He begot no one nor was He begotten. No one is comparable to Him." (112:1-4) There is only one God. He has always existed and will always exist. He does not have progeny, nor is he the progeny of anyone else. And there is no other being like him out there in this universe, any other universe, or anywhere else in existence.

The second doctrine is belief in angels created by God. Angels are intelligent, asexual beings made from light who, without hesitation, do exactly what they're ordered to do. They work for God, doing countless tasks that are needed to run the universe. Satan and his army are jinn, a different type of being, and not angels. There is no concept of fallen angels in Islam. Angels are angels, and jinn are jinn. Angels do not have free will and never disobey God, so they cannot get into a disagreement with him.

The third doctrine is belief in the scriptures. These include the Torah, the Psalms, the Gospels, and any others that may have existed previously. The Qur'an is the final scripture, and there will be none after it, and it exists in its original form as it was revealed and is the word of God. Problems occurred when earlier scriptures were changed with time, but God has promised to protect the Qur'an from corruption. "We have sent down the Qur'an Ourself, and We Our self will guard it." (15:9)

The fourth doctrine is belief in the prophets of God. God sent prophets to all people in all times. They are divided into two categories: messengers and prophets, although the terms are often used interchangeably. Messengers came with a new religion, while prophets came to reinforce a past messenger's teachings. All of them were good, and all of them need to be accepted and respected. The Qur'an names twenty-five messengers and prophets, most of whom are also mentioned in the Bible. Muhammad was the final messenger and prophet, and there will be none after him. The Qur'an says, "Say [Muhammad], 'We [Muslims] believe in God and in what has been sent down to us and to Abraham, Ishmael, Isaac, Jacob, and the Tribes. We believe in what has been given to Moses, Jesus, and the prophets from their Lord. We do not make a distinction between any of the [prophets]. It is to Him that we devote ourselves.'" (3:84)

The fifth doctrine is belief in the Day of Judgment and the afterlife. Humans will be resurrected on the Day of Judgment and will have to answer for all their deeds and will be rewarded in heaven or punished in hell. "He is God: there is no god but Him. He will gather you all together on the Day of Resurrection, about which there is no doubt. Whose word can be truer than God's?" (4:87)

Obligations to God

Duties in Islam are divided between obligations to God and obligations to mankind. Both sets of obligations need to be fulfilled to earn a place in heaven. Here we describe religious obligations that approximate to the obligations we have to God, although some religious obligations, such as charity, are for the benefit of society.

As a Muslim, there are five things you have to do, also called the Pillars of Islam. These are to say the confession of faith, pray five times a day, fast during the month of Ramadan, pay a set amount of charity, and go for the Haj pilgrimage to Mecca at least once in your lifetime.

The first obligation is to say the confession of faith, "There is only one God, and Muhammad is God's messenger." Anyone who says this becomes a Muslim, and this is the only legal requirement for conversion. If you believe these two things, you're already a Muslim. Whoever says the above with full belief and sincerity is guaranteed to go to heaven sooner or later.

The second obligation is to say the five daily prayers. These are set at various times of the day, with the first one being at dawn and the last one late at night. You need to wash yourself and then face Mecca and pray according to an established format that includes reciting verses of the Qur'an. The correct way to say prayers needs to be learned. God says in the Qur'an, "Take care to do your prayers, praying in the best way, and stand before God in devotion." (2:238) If you say all five prayers based on the minimum requirements, it takes about half an hour daily.

God told the Prophet, "I made five daily prayers obligatory on your people, and I guarantee that if anyone observes them regularly at their times, I shall admit him to paradise; if anyone does not offer them regularly, there is no such guarantee for him."[14]

For Christians who would like to know how Jesus might have prayed, the best way to find out is to see how Orthodox Jews say their prayers. After all, Jesus was raised in a Jewish environment and he would have prayed like they do. The interesting thing is that their physical movements of standing, bowing and doing full prostrations are almost exactly the same as the Muslims. You can look it up on YouTube.

The third obligation is that during the lunar month of Ramadan, you need to fast from dawn to dusk. During that time, you cannot eat, drink, smoke, or have sex. People who are not able to fast, for instance due to illness, are exempted. God has promised that those who fast will be especially rewarded by him on the Day of Judgment, as all other forms of worship are meant for the benefit of the worshipper, while fasting is especially reserved for God's sake, and it draws people closer to him. The Qur'an says, "You who believe, fasting is prescribed for you, as it was prescribed for those before you, so that you may be mindful of God." (2:183)

The fourth obligation is to pay a set amount in charity. This is a yearly payment equivalent to 2.5 percent of your net assets. It requires some calculation, but if your average net worth for a year was $100,000, you need to pay about $2,500 for that year, which works out to about $200 per month. If everything you own is worth only $10,000, then you need to pay only $250 per year.

The fifth obligation is that once in your lifetime, if you can afford it and are physically able to, you must go to Mecca for Haj. The annual Haj pilgrimage happens during a specific time of the year.

These are pretty much all the religious obligations there are, and God says in the Qur'an that he's kept things easy for us. "Believers, bow down, prostrate yourselves, worship your Lord, and do good so that you may succeed. Strive hard for God as is His due: He has chosen you and placed no hardship in your religion, the faith of your forefather Abraham." (22:77-78)

The Qur'an says, "Hurry towards your Lord's forgiveness and a Garden as wide as the heavens and earth prepared for the righteous." (3:133)

The Prophet said, "Whoever believes in God and his Apostle, offers prayers perfectly and fasts in the month of Ramadan, then it is incumbent upon God to admit him into paradise."[15]

Obligations to Mankind

The obligations we have to fellow humans are all those things that relate to our dealings with other people and living a decent life; things such as being good with our parents, spouses, family, friends, relatives, neighbors, co-workers, and the world at large. Also included are things such as dealing justly with people, fulfilling our commitments, being charitable, helping the poor, etc. Fulfilling these requirements is for the benefit of the community and society at large. A smoothly functioning society allows individuals living in it to worship God and prolongs the lifespan of the religious order.

Doing good deeds has as much emphasis in Islam as worshipping God. The Qur'an is full of verses urging believers to be good with fellow human beings. "God has promised forgiveness and a rich reward to those who have faith and do good works." (5:9) "But those who believe and do good deeds will be given the Gardens of Paradise." (18:107) This statement of "believing in God and doing righteous deeds" is repeated around fifty times in the Qur'an as a requirement for people to be admitted to heaven. Just believing is not enough to earn heaven; good deeds are just as necessary. Just believing in God but not doing anything good in your life can land you in hell for a while, and not believing in God but doing good deeds can keep you out of heaven forever. Faith and good works are both necessary to go directly to heaven. Good deeds include fulfilling the obligations to both God and man.

Part of doing good is to call others to do what is right and to forbid what is wrong. "Be a community that calls for what is good, urges what is right, and forbids what is wrong: those who do this are the successful ones." (3:104)

Giving in charity, restraining anger, and forgiving people is an important part of being a good person. "Hurry towards your Lord's forgiveness and a Garden as wide as the heavens and earth prepared for the righteous, who give, both in prosperity and adversity, who restrain their anger and pardon people—God loves those who do good." (3:133-134) The Prophet said that God forgives those who forgive others. Conversely, if you can't forgive others, then God will be less inclined towards forgiving you.

The Qur'an says, "Worship God: join nothing with Him. Be good to your parents, to relatives, to orphans, to the needy, to neighbors near and far, to travelers in need, and to your slaves. God does not like arrogant, boastful people, who are miserly and order other people to be the same, hiding the bounty God has given them." (4:36-37)

Of all people, being good to your parents is the most important. "Your Lord has commanded that you should worship none but Him, and that you be kind to your parents. If either or both of them reach old age with you, say no word that shows impatience with them, and do not be harsh with them, but speak to them respectfully and lower your wing in humility towards them in kindness and say, 'Lord, have mercy on them, just as they cared for me when I was little.'" (17:23-24) Even if you're a believer and your parents are not, you're still required to treat them kindly. The only time you are allowed to disobey your parents is if they tell you to worship anyone or anything other than God. There are seven different verses in the Qur'an urging people to be good towards their parents.

Doing justice is very strongly emphasized, even if it means bearing witness against your own family members. "You who believe, uphold justice and bear witness to God, even if it is against yourselves, your parents, or your close relatives. Whether the person is rich or poor, God can best take care of both. Refrain from following your own desire, so that you can act justly—if you distort or neglect justice, God is fully aware of what you do." (4:135)

The Qur'an and Hadith are full of exhortations to do good deeds, not just with humans, but even with animals. How important this is can be gauged from the following story. The Prophet said, "A man saw a dog eating mud from the severity of thirst. So, that man took a shoe and filled it with water and kept on pouring the water for the dog till it quenched its thirst. So God approved of his deed and made him enter Paradise."[16]

The Qur'an says that if we avoid the worst sins, God may forgive smaller ones. "As for those who avoid grave sins and foul acts, though they may commit small sins, your Lord is ample in forgiveness. He has been aware of you from the time He produced you from the earth and from your hiding places in your mother's wombs, so do not assert your own goodness: He knows best who is mindful of Him." (53:32)

Another command that is repeated dozens of times in the Qur'an is to obey God and the Messenger. "God will admit those who obey Him and His Messenger to Gardens graced with flowing streams, and there they will stay—that is the supreme triumph!" (4:13) Obeying the Messenger is equated with obeying God.

The Prophet advised us to avoid seven great sins which are: 1) To worship anything other than God, 2) Magic, 3) Murder, 4) Charging usury, 5) Eating an orphan's wealth, 6) Fleeing from the battlefield, and 7) Scandalizing an innocent woman.[17]

Another time, the Prophet said that the four greatest sins are: 1) To worship anything other than God, 2) Murder, 3) To be undutiful toward one's parents and 4) Giving false witness.

Beyond these sins, there's another long list compiled by scholars of seventy great sins that include sins such as fornication, adultery, lying, and stealing.

Christians may find it interesting to know that the list of sins in Islam is pretty much the same as in Christianity.

The Points System

Everything you do is being recorded. This includes all your actions as well as your thoughts, down to the depths of your subconscious mind. Two angels always accompany you, recording your good and bad deeds. On the Day of Judgment, your record will be presented to you showing all your actions converted into negative or positive points that will then be weighed on a "scale." If your positive points outweigh your negative points, you will go directly to heaven; otherwise you will go to hell, unless God forgives your sins.

The Qur'an talks about two angels always recording your activities as good or bad deeds. "We created man—We know what his soul whispers to him: We are closer to him than his jugular vein—with two receptors [usually taken to mean 'recording angels'] set to record, one on his right side and one on his left: he does not utter a single word without an ever-present watcher." (50:16-18)

"In whatever matter you [Prophet] may be engaged and whatever part of the Qur'an you are reciting, whatever work you [people] are doing, We witness you when you are engaged in it. Not even the weight of a speck of dust in the earth or sky escapes your Lord, nor anything lesser or greater: it is all written in a clear record." (10:61)

Negative actions are written in a record called Sijjin. "Do these people not realize that they will be raised up on a mighty Day, a Day when everyone will stand before the Lord of the Worlds? No indeed! The list of the wicked is in Sijjin—what will explain to you what Sijjin is?—a clearly numbered list." (83:4-9)

Positive actions are written in a record called Illiyyin. "No indeed! The list of the truly good is in Illiyyin—what will explain to you what 'Illiyyin' is?—a clearly written list." (83:18-20)

All your good and bad actions will be converted into numbered points, and then, on the Day of Judgment, they will be weighed on a scale. "We will set up scales of justice for the Day of Resurrection so that no one can be wronged in the least, and if there should be even the weight of a mustard seed, We shall bring it out—We take excellent account." (21:47)

If your positive points are more than your negative points, you will go straight to heaven. "On that Day the weighing of deeds will be true and just: those whose good deeds are heavy on the scales will be the ones to prosper, and those whose good deeds are light will be the ones who have lost their souls through their wrongful rejection of Our messages." (7:8-9)

There's a point system in place, and every activity you do carries positive or negative points. How the point system works is pretty complicated, and I'm not aware of anyone who has even made an attempt to come up with a system for assigning points to the things we do in everyday life so that people might be able to get an idea of what kind of points they are accumulating.

Ever since childhood, I have been told that doing good deeds earns you *sawab*. In Arabic it is pronounced *thawab* and means reward. I have always understood it to mean that you're getting some sort of points, because the way the expression is used, it implies that doing an action that is better than another one earns you more sawab. For example, it is common to say that to pray in a local mosque earns you sawab, but if you say the same prayer in a mosque in Mecca, it might earn you seven hundred times more sawab.

Similarly, doing bad actions earn you *gunah*, which is a Persian word meaning sin. Conversely to sawab, gunah is used in the sense of earning demerit points: "This action will earn you a lot of gunah."

The following is an example of the Prophet using the same concept when he said, "If any one of you follows strictly his Islamic religion, then his good deeds will be rewarded ten times to seven hundred times for each good deed and a bad deed will be recorded as it is."[18]

Therefore, it is clear that good deeds earn you merit points and bad deeds earn you demerit points, and these are the points that will be weighed on the scales on the Day of Judgment.

Scientists and mathematicians have discovered that it is possible to describe all the laws of nature in mathematical equations. Galileo Galilei is reported to have said, "Mathematics is the language with which God wrote the universe." Therefore, it should be no surprise that even good and bad deeds can be converted into numbers using some sort of logical methodology, or algorithm. No one has done it yet, and I'm not aware of anyone having attempted it either. It would be a great topic for researching and writing a PhD thesis or a book.

Since figuring out a precise methodology behind the point system is too large a topic for me to cover in this book, I will just mention some of the major points of how it might work and leave the details for a later time.

The way the point system may work is that you could start off with the smallest good deed and assign it one point, say giving someone a glass of water. Then, as good deeds get bigger and better, they will earn more points, say giving a glass of milk may be five points because milk costs more and is more beneficial to a person, so it earns the giver several times as many points as giving a glass of water.

Things can begin to get a little bit more complicated when you start adding other factors to the act of giving a glass of water. Say you're in a desert with very little water, but you still give a glass of water to a fellow traveler who has run out. Now your act of giving a glass of water might earn you one hundred times as many points as doing the same thing at home, where water is plentiful.

Similarly, a poor person giving $100 in charity may earn more points than a millionaire giving $1,000, because that $100 is worth a lot more to a poor person than $1,000 is to a millionaire. Therefore, the circumstances of an action influence the number of points you earn.

Adding intentions behind an act will also determine the number of merit points you will earn. If you gave the glass of water purely for helping out the other person and earning God's approval, that would be considered a good thing and earn you merit points. But if you did so because you expect to get something in return, then your intentions were mixed, and the act will have less value. It might earn you less than one full point. Doing a good deed in order to please God, or to help a fellow human being out of sympathy, is considered better than doing the same thing for worldly benefit.

The greater the deed, the more points you get and vice versa. The greatest deed you can do is to give your life for the sake of God, and it catapults you to the highest levels of heaven, no questions asked. But if your intentions were mixed, such as dying for glory, then that invalidates your sacrifice. There is a hadith describing a person on the Day of Judgment who will claim to have died for God and will be told that he actually died to be praised by men, and it is said that he will be sent to hell.[19]

Assuming that intentions for all the deeds you do are good, then there are many deeds you can do that will earn you a large number of points. We have mentioned earlier the story of a person giving water to a thirsty dog and earning so many points for it that he got sent to heaven for that one deed.

Many years ago, I did some Microsoft computer science exams, and the way the tests were scored was not based on how many questions you got right, but rather it was graded based on the most difficult question you could solve. It is called computerized adaptive testing. If you answer one question correctly, you are presented with a more difficult question. If you solve that, you are given an even more difficult question, and so on. If you get a question wrong, then you are given an easier question. If you answer that correctly, you are again given a more difficult question. Finally, the computer program figures out your grade based on the most difficult questions you have the ability to answer.

Sometimes it seems like God is also testing us based on the very best actions we are capable of doing. If we do some good deed that is outstanding, then we seem to get a special reward for that. This can be inferred from the following quote from the Qur'an, where God is telling us that he's looking at our best actions. "What you have runs out but what God has endures, and We shall certainly reward those who remain steadfast according to the best of their actions. To whoever, male or female, does good deeds and has faith, We shall give a good life and reward them according to the best of their actions." (16:96-97)

All our activities are being recorded and scored, but those deeds we do that stand out in their merit are especially counted in our final report card. The Qur'an mentions this in another place also, "If they spend a little or a lot for God's cause, if they traverse a mountain pass, all this is recorded to their credit so that God can reward them in accordance with the best of their deeds." (9:121)

The way I see it, if two people have accumulated the same overall number of positive points and both are going to heaven, but one of them has some "spikes" of points because of doing some deeds of outstanding merit, then that person will likely earn a place in a higher grade of heaven out of the hundred or more grades.

If we were making a chart of the sort of points you get for each deed, we can make a list of the very best deeds in descending order of merit, with the best deed getting one million points and the least deed getting one point. Then, we would need to add two more variables to get a proper weight for an action at the moment when that deed was done. One is the circumstances of the action, such as whether it was very easy for you to do or very difficult, and the second variable is your intention at the time of doing the action. So, giving someone a glass of water may earn you anywhere from 0.1 to 100 points.

The same logic applies to bad actions. If you hit someone out of anger, you might earn 100 negative points, but if you hit them by a careless mistake, you may get only 10 negative points. But let's say the circumstance was that you were an adult and hit a child to steal their candy, then you might get 100,000 negative points.

The worst possible act you can do is not to believe in God or to worship someone other than God. In that case, you may get an infinite number of negative points; so many that no good you can possibly do will save you from hell. In that case, any good deeds you do will only earn you a place in a higher level of hell; hell also has multiple levels, and higher levels are less painful than lower ones.

God has made the way points are counted biased in favor of earning positive points. The Prophet said, "God has written down the good deeds and the bad ones. He who has intended a good deed and has not done it, God writes it down with himself as a full good deed, but if he has intended it and has done it, God writes it down with himself as from ten good deeds to seven hundred times, or many times over. But if he has intended a bad deed and has not done it, God writes it down with himself as a full good deed, but if he has intended it and has done it, God writes it down as one bad deed."[20]

If you intend to do a good deed and actually do it, you get from ten to seven hundred or more merit points.

If you intend to do a good deed but do not do it, you get one merit point.

If you intend to do a bad deed and do not do it, you still get one merit point.

If you intend to do a bad deed and actually do it, you get one demerit point.

On the Day of Judgment, you will be presented with your Record of Deeds, and you will find that the tiniest good or bad thing you did will be in it. "The record of their deeds will be laid open and you will see the guilty, dismayed at what they contain, saying, 'Woe to us! What a record this is! It does not leave any deed, small or large, unaccounted for!' They will find everything they ever did laid in front of them: your Lord will not be unjust to anyone." (18:49)

On the Day of Judgment, if a person has hurt someone, some of his merit points will be given to the victim as compensation. Even if he hurt someone by telling a joke about him and laughing at him, some of his points will go to the other person. If he has harmed many people, it is possible that all his merit points could end up being given away and he could be left with zero merit points. In that case, if there are still some people left whom he has harmed, then their demerit points will be transferred to him, and his count of negative points will increase.[21]

God's justice is absolute, and he will not let the least good action go to waste. Every single thing you do is going to be repaid, even if it means getting an extra tree in heaven, or the alleviation of a little pain in hell. Even the tiniest action will be transformed into a benefit or punishment.

Your rank in heaven will depend on how many good points you have accumulated. "Everyone is assigned a rank according to their deeds; your Lord is not unaware of anything they do." (6:132)

Satan's Challenge to God

There are so many challenges facing us in this world that prevent us from fulfilling our purpose in life and going to heaven. One of the biggest obstacles is Satan and his army, who are determined to destroy as many of us as they can out of spite and hatred that God created us and honored us more than them. They can't hurt God, but they take their rage out on us.

As we struggle to live up to God's expectations, we need to keep in mind that we're constantly under attack from a source that most people are unaware of.

Let us recall that Adam and Eve were created to live in a perfect environment. They were expelled from heaven because Satan misled them into disobeying God, and now Satan and the other jinn under his control are constantly assaulting us by inserting negative thoughts into our minds. We need to remember this because our real battle in this world is against Satan and his army, not against each other.

To know what game is being played in this world, we need to go back to the beginning of this book where we talked about the creation of Adam and how Satan rebelled. Recall that Satan was a jinn living among angels, and when God created Adam and asked the angels to bow down to him, Satan refused. "God said, 'What prevented you from bowing down as I commanded you?'

and he said, 'I am better than him: You created me from fire and him from clay.' God said, 'Get down from here! This is no place for your arrogance. Get out! You are contemptible!' but Iblis said, 'Give me respite until the Day people are raised from the dead,' and God replied, 'You have respite.' And then Iblis said, 'Because You have put me in the wrong, I will lie in wait for them all on Your straight path: I will come at them—from their front and their back, from their right and their left—and You will find that most of them are ungrateful.' God said, 'Get out! You are disgraced and banished! I swear I shall fill Hell with you and all who follow you!'" (7:12-18) Iblis is the Arabic name for Lucifer.

Another chapter of the Qur'an describes it as such, "Iblis then said to God, 'Because You have put me in the wrong, I will lure mankind on earth and put them in the wrong, all except Your devoted servants.' God said, '[Devotion] is a straight path to Me: you will have no power over My servants, only over the ones who go astray and follow you.'" (15:39-42)

Satan blames God for his own rebellious behavior. God may or may not have agreed with Satan's logic about who was superior: Satan or Adam, but he was angry at Satan's refusal to obey his command. Unlike angels, Satan had free will that allowed him to obey or disobey God, and he chose to disobey, and no one gets away with disobeying God unless they repent. Although the Qur'an does not mention it, there have been suggestions that God allowed Satan time to repent, but he refused; such was his anger at God's creation of humans. In contrast, Adam and Eve repented after they had disobeyed God and eaten the forbidden fruit and were forgiven.

Humanity is divided into two groups: those who follow Satan and those who are servants of God, immune from being led astray. That is the greater struggle going on between good and evil, and the hope is that we will manage to be counted in the camp of God instead of the camp of Satan.

Satan's Method of Attack

The method Satan uses to lead people astray is to enter suggestions into their subconscious minds through "whispering." This is similar to a hypnotist inserting suggestions into a person's mind.

When Adam and Eve were in heaven, in the Qur'anic version of the story, Satan whispered into their ears, and not necessarily appeared physically. "But Satan whispered to Adam, saying, 'Adam, shall I show you the tree of immorality and power that never decays?' and they both ate from it." (20:120-121)

"Satan whispered to them so as to expose their nakedness, which had been hidden from them: he said, 'Your

Lord only forbade you this tree to prevent you becoming angels or immortals,' and he swore to them, 'I am giving you sincere advice'—he lured them with lies." (7:20-22)

What the whispering of Satan means is that an idea occurs to our minds that is contrary to goodness and we imagine it to be an outcome of logic that we've thought up ourselves. But it's really a suggestion that's been planted into our subconscious mind by an external entity, similar to how a hypnotist can plant suggestions into a person's subconscious.

Jinn are an intelligent species of beings that live on this earth. Scientists are forever looking for intelligent life in the universe, but they neglect this species that already lives here. They're made of "smokeless fire," which is some form of energy. Some people say that they're made from electromagnetic energy in the infrared spectrum. They are intelligent and have free will like humans. Not all of them are bad, with some being followers of God, but Satan's army of demons consists of jinn, and they consider humans to be their enemies and conduct their war by entering negative thoughts into our minds. They instigate wars, marriage breakdowns, broken friendships, criminal activity, and pretty much all the evil that we see.

Jinn are interdimensional beings, able to pop in and out of this dimension, and are usually hidden from view, although they can materialize in various forms and have the ability to become visible. The Qur'an says, "Children of Adam, do not let Satan seduce you, as he did your parents, causing them to leave the Garden, stripping them of their garments to expose their nakedness to them: he and his forces can see you from where you cannot see them: We have made evil ones allies to those who do not believe." (7:27) Jinn can see us, but we cannot see them, which gives them an advantage over us.

Each human has a jinn assigned to him by Satan, whispering suggestions into his mind.[22] This jinn is in the command of Satan, and his job is to corrupt a person with negative thoughts.

It is hard to judge whether, if Satan and his army were not trying to corrupt people, all humans would have been good and saintly or not. It is possible that many people would still have been bad, but maybe not as many people and maybe not as bad. Just to throw a hypothetical figure, maybe if Satan had not existed, twenty-five percent of humans may have turned out bad, but with Satan attacking us, ninety percent became corrupted.

We need not be afraid of Satan and jinn. All they can do is enter wrong suggestions into our minds; otherwise they have no power over us. We also have guardian angels protecting us, and people who are truly good escape from the control of Satan altogether.

Advice for Christians

The Qur'an says, "The [Muslim] believers, the Jews, the Christians, and the Sabians—all those who believe in God and the Last Day and do good—will have their rewards with their Lord. No fear for them, nor will they grieve." (2:62)

Prophet Muhammad said, "I am most akin to Jesus Christ among the whole of mankind, and all the prophets are of different mothers but belong to one religion and no prophet was raised between me and Jesus."[23]

I have lived most of my life in the West among Christians, and I'm hoping that many Christians will read this book, even if only to find out the Islamic perspective of heaven. Therefore, I would like to discuss what the Qur'an says about Christianity as it pertains to going to heaven. Because my intention is to help everyone go to heaven, instead of trying to be politically correct and fudge things, I'm going to state exactly what the Qur'an and Hadith say.

I have previously quoted the Qur'an saying that God does not forgive the sin of worshipping anyone other than God. "God does not forgive the joining of partners with Him: anything less than that He forgives to whoever He will, but anyone who joins partners with God has concocted a tremendous sin." (4:48)

God himself is talking to us in the Qur'an, and he does not want Jesus to be worshipped as an equal to

God. "Those who say, 'God is the Messiah, son of Mary,' have defied God. The Messiah himself said, 'Children of Israel, worship God, my Lord and your Lord.' If anyone associates others with God, God will forbid him from the Garden, and Hell will be his home. No one will help such evildoers." (5:72)

That is about as clear as it can get. Jesus is supposed to be a human being and a prophet; one of the greatest prophets there were and deserving of the utmost respect, but if he is raised to the status of God and worshipped, it is not something God takes kindly to.

In another place, the Qur'an says, "People of the Book, do not go to excess in your religion, and do not say anything about God except the truth: the Messiah, Jesus, son of Mary, was nothing more than a messenger of God, His word, directed to Mary, a spirit from Him. So believe in God and His messengers and do not speak of a 'Trinity'—stop [this], that is better for you—God is only one God, He is far above having a son, everything in the heavens and earth belongs to Him and He is the best one to trust. The Messiah would never disdain to be a servant of God, nor would the angels who are close to Him." (4:171-172)

God told the Prophet. "The son of Adam denied me and he had no right to do so. And he reviled me and he had no right to do so. As for his denying me, it is his saying: 'He will not remake me as he made me at first'—and the initial creation of him is no easier for me than remaking him. As for his reviling me, it is his saying: 'God has taken to himself a son,' while I am the one, the everlasting refuge. I begot not nor was I begotten, and there is none comparable to me."[24]

Jesus's high standing with God is not in doubt, and the Qur'an makes it clear that Jesus was one of the greatest prophets of God. Here the Qur'an is talking about the angels visiting Mary and telling her, "Mary, God gives you news of a Word from Him, whose name will be the Messiah, Jesus, son of Mary, who will be held in honour in this world and the next, who will be one of those brought near to God. He will speak to people in his infancy and in this adulthood. He will be one of the righteous." (3:45-46)

God asks Christians to stop worshipping Jesus and ask for forgiveness. "Those people who say that God is the third of three are defying [the truth]: there is only One God. If they persist in what they are saying, a painful punishment will afflict those of them who persist. Why do they not turn to God and ask for His forgiveness, when God is most forgiving, most merciful? The Messiah, son of Mary, was only a messenger; other messengers had come and gone before him; his mother was a virtuous woman; both ate food [like other mortals].

See how clear We make these signs for them; see how deluded they are." (5:73-75)

On the Day of Judgment, God will ask Jesus if he claimed to be God. "When God says, 'Jesus, son of Mary, did you say to people. "Take me and my mother as two gods alongside God"?' he will say, 'May You be exalted! I would never say what I had no right to say—if I had said such a thing You would have known it: You know all that is within me, though I do not know what is within You, You alone have full knowledge of things unseen—I told them only what You commanded me to: "Worship God, my Lord and your Lord." I was a witness over them during my time among them. Ever since You took my soul, You alone have been the watcher over them: You are witness to all things and if You punish them, they are Your servants; if You forgive them, You are the Almighty, the Wise.'" (5:116-118)

When Jesus says, "if You punish them, they are Your servants; if You forgive them, You are the Almighty, the Wise," he will be hoping that God will forgive his followers.

Christianity and Islam spring from the same roots, going back to Abraham and his progeny. While the prophets of Judaism and Christianity were descendants of Abraham's son Isaac, Muhammad was a descendent of Abraham's other son, Ishmael.

The two religions share the vast majority of beliefs, and I would go so far as to say that they are ninety percent the same. Both teach belief in God, angels, prophets, scriptures, and the afterlife. This is as near as any two religions can get.

The main theological difference between them is regarding the nature of God and Jesus. At some point in its history, Christianity adopted a belief in the divinity of Jesus and elevated him to the status of being the Son of God, or part of a Trinity. Studying history, it seems that this was not always the case, and in the early days, there were many churches with varying views, including the belief that Jesus was a prophet. It was only during the time of Emperor Constantine, around 300 AD, that it was decided to officially declare the divinity of Jesus and to suppress contrary views.

Jesus says in the Bible, "Be perfect, therefore, as your heavenly Father is perfect." (Matthew 5:48) If Jesus claimed to be God or the Son of God, then he himself would be without fault and he would say, "Be perfect, like I am perfect," but he didn't claim that.

It would be wrong to say that Christianity stands or falls on the belief in the divinity of Jesus. Even today there are Christians who believe in Jesus as a human being and a prophet, like the Unitarians. Many famous people have been Unitarians, including some of the Founding Fathers of the United States, for instance John Adams and Thomas Jefferson. Interestingly, Thomas Jefferson had a copy of the Qur'an, as portrayed in the book titled *Thomas Jefferson's Qur'an: Islam and the Founders* by Denise A. Spellberg.[25]

The purpose of this book is to describe heaven and the means to get there. The ultimate purpose of life has been described as getting into heaven, which is the supreme triumph for a person. My own advice to Christians who are reading this, the same as to Muslims, is to focus all your efforts towards that goal. Whatever takes you closer to the goal of entering heaven is good, and whatever takes you away from it is to be avoided. At the minimum, start believing in a unitary God and do not mix up God's being with anything or anyone else. Don't take the risk of facing God on the Day of Judgment and being asked whom you worshipped. Consider Jesus as a great man, one of the greatest prophets, and give him as much respect as you do now, but worship God alone. Remember what I said earlier—that if you believe in one God, you will go to heaven—that's a promise.[26]

Intercession

The subject of intercession is a long one, but I will briefly describe how it works because it is one way of getting people out of hell and into heaven, even if they haven't earned it.

The way it will work is that God will allow some people who are the closest to him to intercede on behalf of those people who have been sent to hell because they did not have enough good deeds to be admitted to heaven. Even though those people may get out of hell one day on their own merit, they will be taken out much sooner through intercession.

God says in the Qur'an, "Who is there that can intercede with Him except by His leave?" (2:255) Also, "There are many angels in heaven whose intercession will be of no use until God gives permission to those He will, whose words He will accept." (53:26) What these verses are referring to is that a person can intercede on behalf of someone else only with God's permission. It is part of God's mercy that he will allow some people to be removed from hell earlier than they deserve.

The Prophet said that God gave him the choice between automatically admitting half of his followers to heaven or giving him the right to intercede on their behalf on the Day of Judgment. He chose intercession, presumably in the hope that he would be able to get more people out of hell in that way.[27]

The position in heaven referred to in Chapter 4, called *Al-Wasilah*, that only one person will get, will give that person the right to intercede with God on behalf of the largest number of sinners. The Prophet hoped that, on the

Day of Judgment, God would grant that position to him and give him the right to intercede for a set number of people and, as long as they believed in God, the Prophet said that he would intercede for them and they would be removed from hell.

Other prophets will also be given the right to intercede for a certain number of their own followers. Even common people who have a good standing with God will be able to extricate some people out of hell. The Prophet said, "There will be from my community such as will intercede for many groups of people, such as will intercede for a tribe, such as will intercede for a clan, and such as will intercede for just one man, until they enter paradise."[28]

It is, therefore, possible for anyone to acquire from God the privilege to intercede on behalf of others. If you pray for it, God may grant you the privilege, and you might be able to save one or more loved ones from hell and have them transferred to heaven.

The only condition is that the person on whose behalf you are interceding must have believed in God, otherwise intercession will not be accepted. The Prophet himself will not be able to save some members of his family who did not believe, including his own mother, who died as a pagan, while he was still very young.[29]

The best way to help people you love to enter heaven is to persuade them to believe in God and to do good deeds. If you cannot convince them, or if they've already passed away, then the best thing to do is to pray for them, give charity on their behalf, and to raise your own status with God so high that he grants you the right to intercede for them on the Day of Judgment.

Summary of How to Get into Heaven

If we were to compile a comprehensive list of things you should do and things that you should avoid in order to get into heaven, it can easily run into hundreds of items. In order to simplify things a bit, we will summarize the major points.

The first and most important thing you have to do is to believe that God exists and that there is only one, indivisible God.

You should follow up that belief by fulfilling your obligations to God, which consist of 1) Saying the confession of faith, 2) Praying five times a day, 3) Fasting in Ramadan, 4) Giving the prescribed charity, and 5) Going for Haj once in your lifetime.

Thirdly, you should avoid the great sins and do as many good deeds as possible. If you avoid the major sins and do at least a minimum of good deeds, you will avoid hell and earn a place in heaven. If you worship God more, avoid even small sins, and do extra good deeds, then your status will be raised in the eyes of God and you will earn a place in a higher grade of heaven.

12

Conclusion

Getting into heaven requires effort. You have a much better chance of making it if you work towards it and do the required work. Not only should we hope for heaven, we should be aspiring for the highest grade possible.

Knowing the details of what heaven is like is a great way of motivating ourselves to make the effort required to get there. Let's use the analogy of going to college. If you were applying to a university, it is likely that you would do some research on available universities. You might get a book on university rankings and try to get admitted into the best one possible. Maybe, if you have high aims, you might want to try for one of the top universities, such as Harvard or Stanford. Once you have selected the one you want to go to, you will make your best effort to meet its requirements for admission, studying hard to get good grades in high school, taking part in extracurricular activities, and so on. You would probably need to take the SAT, and you would spend a lot of time studying for it. While working hard, you would be motivated by the expectation of the benefits you will be getting from going to that particular university. Not only will you enjoy going there, but you will also earn a valuable degree, and it will help you get a job and help you in your career for the rest of your life.

Going to heaven is like being admitted to a university. If you can spend time doing research on a university where you will be going for four years, you need to spend much more time finding out about heaven, where you will be going for billions of years. Going to a top university is like going to a higher grade in heaven. Studying hard for meeting admission requirements is like living in this world and doing what is necessary for going to heaven. Being shut out of heaven is like not getting into any university.

University students are an elite group, and if we count all the school students in the world, most of them will never attend college. Some won't get the opportunity. Some won't make the effort, and some will make some effort, but still won't get in. Similarly, only a minority of humans will make it to heaven, because many will not be interested and will never make any effort to go there, and some may make some effort, but will fail because they didn't bother finding out what exactly was required to get there.

The main point I want to make by using the analogy of admission to college is that the desire to go to a chosen university will provide you with motivation when you're working hard to meet its entrance requirements. If you were studying for the SAT and hadn't made up your mind about whether you even wanted to go to college, then chances were that you didn't make as much effort to do well as you might have if you had a specific university in mind and wanted to meet their minimum requirements. Similarly, if you do not know what heaven is like and you have no major desire to go there, then chances are that you will not make the effort that is required. Therefore, it is of the utmost importance to know as many details about heaven as possible, so that it will motivate you to make the required effort.

Universities have long lists of requirements for admission, and so does heaven. We may not like the strict criteria set by universities, especially the top ones, but we know that there's nothing we can do to change them, and we comply—we do what is required instead of arguing with the university admissions office about their requirements. Similarly, we cannot take heaven for granted and expect that we'll just walk in there. We can grumble if we want to about the list of requirements for admission to heaven, but there's nothing we can do to change it, and we have no choice but to comply.

Let me give you another example of how we willingly comply with laws in this world. Suppose you wanted to visit a country and needed a visa. You have to comply with that country's laws and provide its authorities with the required documents and meet their criteria for issuing a visa, otherwise, they'll deny you entry, and no amount of tantrums you throw will change their minds. So why should God allow us into heaven if we refuse to comply with his requirements?

Unlike universities, which have limited places available, God has made heaven not just big enough for every human who has ever been born, but big enough for the inhabitants of hundreds of other worlds. There's no shortage of space, but because many people will refuse to go there, by not complying with God's requirements, the places that remain unfilled in heaven will be divided among those who enter it.

If someone doesn't even believe in God or the afterlife, then there's not much I can do to change their minds, as it is outside the scope of this book to try to prove the existence of God and heaven. All I can say is that I believe in heaven one hundred percent myself, and I believe that everything I have said in this book is true, and I'm prepared to make the necessary effort to go there.

For me, heaven is not a distant, hypothetical place; rather, I imagine it to be close by, practically on the other side of the wall. At any given moment in time, I could be seconds away from death and could wake up on the Day of Resurrection feeling like I've slept for only a few hours.

I have written this book with my own sons, nephews, and nieces in mind, and I hope they're among those who believe and will make the required effort to go to heaven. I have also kept in mind a dear Christian friend who is very interested in knowing more details about the afterlife and who has encouraged me to write this book. Beyond my family and friends, my motivation is to instill the desire for heaven in as many people as possible, so that they, too, will do whatever it takes to go there.

This life is like an entrance exam for heaven, and all your life's effort needs to be directed towards getting admission. The stakes are very high, as there are only two places you can go to—heaven or hell. There's no third place, and annihilation is not one of the available options either. If you don't get into a university, you can still get a job, but if you fail to enter heaven, you're going to land in hell for a long time, if not forever.

If you believe in God and do the required work, then God will make your existing life easier, and your death experience will also be pleasant. "This is the way God rewards the righteous, those whose lives the angels take in a state of goodness. They will say to them, 'Peace be upon you. Enter the Garden as a reward for what you have done.'" (16:31-32)

Sooner or later we're all going to experience the moment of death, no matter how young or fit we consider ourselves to be right now. If we've done the right things in life by believing in God and doing good deeds, then that moment could be a pleasant one, as angels will greet us and we'll be on our way to heaven. I myself await that moment with anticipation because I have a great desire to see what heaven is actually like, assuming, of course, that I qualify for it.

I urge everyone to read about near-death experiences to get an idea of what they're like, but I would also like to remind you that NDEs are only about a short period of consciousness after death, and once you cross the barrier of death, then you're going to fall into a state of sleep and wake up on the Day of Judgment. That day, it will feel like you've just woken up after a few hours of sleep from the moment of death.

For believers, the Day of Judgment will be made a lot less unpleasant, as angels will greet them when they get up in their new physical bodies. "They will have no fear of the great Terror: the angels will receive them with the words, 'This is the Day you were promised!'" (21:103)

The judgment process will be made easy for good people: "Whoever is given his record in his right hand will have an easy reckoning and return to his people well pleased." (84:7-9)

For good people, all three major stages we have to go through before entering heaven, namely death, resurrection, and judgment, will be made easier. Even the Prophet used to pray for God to make these things easy for him.

Once the judgment is over, that will be the moment when you will be on your way to heaven. You will cross the As-Sirat Bridge and find yourself at the gates of heaven. There you will find all your family, friends, and relatives who are also headed for heaven.

Then, you'll get to meet Prophet Muhammad and other prophets and drink from the Cistern of Kauthar, and next, you'll be heading for the gates of heaven. Before entering, you'll drink from a stream that will take away all negativity from your soul, and then you'll take a bath in a stream that will transform your body. When you get out of the stream, you'll be dressed like a king or queen, and angels will greet you telling you what a wonderful job you've done to be rewarded with heaven.

As you enter the gates of heaven, you will be met with transport vehicles made from precious materials such as red rubies or emeralds, and they'll fly you to a welcoming banquet and after that to your new home in heaven.

You will find that all of heaven is made from precious materials such as pearls, rubies, diamonds, emeralds, gold, and silver, and even the ground will be littered with gemstones. The biggest shock will be the size and beauty of your mansion and the vast spaciousness of your home grounds. When you enter your mansion, houris and ghilman will greet you, and you'll finally find yourself at home where you always knew you belonged.

You will meet God on a regular basis, and that will be the supreme happiness of your life in heaven. You will live a life of luxury, but your greatest desire will be to see God again. Thinking about your last meeting and waiting in anticipation for the next one will be how you will spend the time in between one meeting and the next.

"But those who believe and do good deeds—and We do not burden any soul with more than it can bear—are the people of the Garden and there they will remain. We shall have removed all ill feeling from their hearts; streams will flow at their feet. They will say, 'Praise be to God, who has guided us to this: had God not guided us, We would never have found the way. The messengers of our Lord brought the Truth.' A voice will call out to them, 'This is the Garden you have been given as your own on account of your deeds.'" (7:42-43)

Endnotes

Providing references for verses in the Qur'an is easy because the numbering system is universally uniform, and all editions of the book use the same chapter and verse numbers. On the other hand, this consistency does not exist in Hadith collections, and various editions sometimes use different numbers for the same hadith.

Most of the Hadith references I've provided have been obtained from three major sources. Two are online websites, muflihun.com and searchtruth.com, that have searchable Hadith databases, and the third is a website, kalamullah.com, where you can find copies of all the major Hadith collections. The editions that I've used are listed in the Bibliography. If you're trying to locate a hadith that I've referenced, then first search for it in muflihun.com or searchtruth.com, and if you don't find it there, then search the books from kalamullah.com.

Introduction

1. The capitalized word "Hadith" denotes the corpus of literature, and "hadith(s)" indicates specific narratives attributed to the Prophet.
2. Al-Jawziyyah, Ibn Qayyim (circa. 1340). Arabic. French translation by Bousserouel, Hebri, *Le Paradis*: Hadi El Arwah ila biladi El Af'rah, Paris: Ed. Universel (2004).

Chapter 1

1. Muslim, Book 32, Hadith 6325; Muslim, Book 40, Hadith 6809
2. Qur'an verses 4:13, 5:119, 6:16, 9:20, 9:72, 9:89, 9:100, 9:111, 10:64, 23:111, 33:71, 37:60, 39:61, 40:9, 44:57, 45:30, 48:5, 57:12, 59:20, 61:12, 64:9, 78:31, 85:11
3. Qur'an verse 72:11
4. Ibn Majah, Book 37, Hadith 4341

Chapter 2

1. Albani, Silsilat al-Hadith as-Saheehah, 3/74, Hadith 1087
2. Bukhari, Book 87, Hadith 116
3. Muslim, Book 40, Hadith 6867
4. Muslim, Book 40, Hadith 6863
5. Bukhari, Book 76, Hadith 522
6. Bukhari, Book 23, Hadith 422
7. Bukhari, Book 3, Hadith 86
8. Bukhari, Book 76, Hadith 522; Muslim Book 40, Hadith 6857
9. Dawood, Book 14, Hadith 2515
10. Muslim, Book 20, Hadith 4651; Dawood, Book 14, Hadith 2514
11. Tafsir Ibn Kathir, Surah 19:62; Ahmed 2390; Saheeh al-Jaami' as-Sagheer, 3/235, Hadith 3636
12. Bukhari, Book 87, Hadith 171
13. Bukhari, Book 23, Hadith 464
14. Bukhari Book 2, Hadith 47

15. Bukhari, Book 23, Hadith 355
16. Al-Nasai, Book 21, Hadith 1834

Chapter 3

1. Muslim, Book 5, Hadith 2161
2. Bukhari, Book 54, Hadith 422
3. Al-Ghazali (circa. 1094). *The Remembrance of Death and the Afterlife: Book XL of the Revival of the Religious Sciences.* Translation: Winter, T. J. Cambridge: Islamic Texts Society (1989).
4. Ibn e Majah, Book 1, Hadith 198
5. Bukhari, Book 60, Hadith 457; Muslim, Book 41, Hadith 7055
6. Bukhari, Book 2, Hadith 47
7. Muslim, Book 20, Hadith 4721
8. Tirmidhi, Book 12, Hadith 2530
9. Bukhari, Book 60, Hadith 457; Muslim, Book 41, Hadith 7056
10. Bukhari, Book 60, Hadith 264; Muslim, Book 40, Hadith 6844
11. Bukhari, Book 76, Hadith 534
12. Bukhari, Book 76, Hadith 538
13. Bukhari, Book 24, Hadith 553
14. Bukhari, Book 60, Hadith 242; Bukhari, Book 12, Hadith 770
15. Bukhari, Book 93, Hadith 532; Muslim, Book 1, Hadith 352
16. Ibn Majah, Book 37, Hadith 4321
17. Bukhari, Book 73, Hadith 29
18. Bukhari, Book 73, Hadith 28
19. Bukhari, Book 76, Hadith 565
20. Bukhari, Book 76, Hadith 564; Bukhari Book 76, Hadith 571

Chapter 4

1. Bukhari, Book 52, Hadith 48; Tirmidhi, Book 36, Hadith 2531
2. Bukhari Book 93, Hadith 481; Yahya, H. *Jannah: The Garden from the Qur'an and Hadith.* London: Ta-Ha. (2007). (Ahmad

Diya ad-Din al- Kamushkhanawi, Ramuz al-Ahadith, vol. 1, p. 30/5).
3. Bukhari, Book 76, Hadith 561
4. Muslim, Book 32, Hadith 6246
5. Yahya, H. *Jannah: The Garden from the Qur'an and Hadith*. London: Ta-Ha. (2007). (Ahmad Diya ad-Din al-Kamushkhanawi, Ramuz al-Ahadith, vol. 2, p. 366/4)
6. Ibn Taymiyyah, Majmu' Fataawa Shaikh al-Islaam, 4/312
7. Tirmidhi, Book 36, Hadith 2538
8. Bukhari, Book 52, Hadith 48; Ibn Majah, Book 37, Hadith 4331
9. Bukhari, Book 11, Hadith 588; Bukhari, Book 60, Hadith 242
10. Al-Nasai, Book 7, Hadith 679
11. Bukhari, Book 52, Hadith 48; Ibn Majah, Book 37, Hadith 4331
12. Qur'an, Surah 56, verses 1-14
13. Bukhari, Book 93, Hadith 536
14. Muslim, Book 4, Hadith 1581
15. Al-Jawziyyah, Ibn Qayyim (circa. 1340). Arabic. French translation by Bousserouel, Hebri. *Le Paradis: Hadi El Arwah ila biladi El Af'rah*. Paris: Ed. Universel (2004).
16. Ibid.
17. Kitab at-Tabaqat al-Kabir, Muhammed Ibn Sa'd
18. Ibn e Majah, Book 37, 4336
19. Bukhari, Book 54, Hadith 414; Muslim, Book 33, Hadith 6416
20. Bukhari, Book 54, Hadith 416; Bukhari Book 93, Hadith 501; Muslim, Book 37, Hadith 6626
21. Muslim, Book 33, Hadith 6402; Tirmidhi, Book 25, Hadith 2516
22. Roohul Ma'ani Vol. 6 p. 49

Chapter 5
1. Tirmidhi, Book 36, Hadith 2553
2. Muslim, Book 42, Hadith 7134

3. Bukhari Book 2, Hadith 47
4. Bukhari, Book 54, Hadith 440
5. Bukhari, Book 54, Hadith 459
6. Bukhari, Book 60, Hadith 378; Bukhari, Book 60, Hadith 379
7. Qur'an, Verses 56:17; 76:19
8. Qur'an, Verse 52:24
9. Tirmidhi, Book 36, Hadith 2562
10. Al-Jawziyyah, Ibn Qayyim (circa. 1340). Arabic. French translation by Bousserouel, Hebri. *Le Paradis: Hadi El Arwah ila biladi El Af'rah*. Paris: Ed. Universel. (2004).
11. Bukhari, Book 54, Hadith 469; Muslim, Book 40, Hadith 6793
12. Ibn e Majah, Book 9, Hadith 2014
13. Al-Jawziyyah, Ibn Qayyim (circa. 1340). Arabic. French translation by Bousserouel, Hebri. *Le Paradis: Hadi El Arwah ila biladi El Af'rah*. Paris: Ed. Universel. (2004); Al-Ghazali (circa. 1094). *The Remembrance of Death and the Afterlife: Book XL of the Revival of the Religious Sciences*. Translation: Winter, T. J. Cambridge: Islamic Texts Society. (1989).
14. Tabarani
15. Bukhari, Book 52, Hadith 53
16. Al-Qurtubi. *At-Tadhkirah*. Translated by Bedeir, R. El-Mansoura: Dar Al-Manarah (Chapter 122, Hadith 414).
17. Ibid. (Chapter 122, Hadith 414).
18. Ibid. (Chapter 122, Hadith 413).
19. Tirmidhi, Book 36, Hadith 2564
20. Albani, Al-Silsilat al-Saheehah, no. 1966
21. Ibn e Majah, Book 12, Hadith 2306
22. Yahya, H. (2007). *Jannah: The Garden from the Qur'an and Hadith*. London: Ta-Ha. (Ahmad Diya ad-Din al-Kamushkhanawi, Ramuz al-Ahadith, vol. 1, p. 30/5).

Chapter 6

1. Bukhari, Book 43, Hadith 620
2. Bukhari, Book 71, Hadith 648
3. Bukhari, Book 88, Hadith 172; Muslim Book 30, Hadith 5701
4. Muslim, Book 30, Hadith 5701
5. Muslim Book 30, Hadith 5702
6. Tirmidhi, Book 35, Hadith 2433
7. Bukhari, Book 88, Hadith 172
8. Tirmidhi, Book 35, Book 2443
9. Bukhari, Book 71, Hadith 648
10. Tirmidhi, Book 36, Hadith 2458
11. Bukhari, Book 31, Hadith 121
12. Bukhari, Book 55, Hadith 644; Muslim Book 1, Hadith 43
13. Al-Jawziyyah, Ibn Qayyim (circa. 1340). Arabic. French translation by Bousserouel, Hebri *Le* Paradis: Hadi El Arwah ila biladi El Af'rah. Paris: Ed. Universel. (2004); Al-Ghazali (circa. 1094). *The Remembrance of Death and the Afterlife: Book XL of the Revival of the Religious Sciences.* Translation: Winter, T. J. Cambridge: Islamic Texts Society. (1989); Al-Qurtubi. *At-Tadhkirah.* Translated by Bedeir, R. El-Mansoura: Dar Al-Manarah (Chapter 137, Hadith 447).
14. Bukhari, Book 55, Hadith 544; Muslim, Book 40, Hadith 6809
15. Bukhari, Book 55, Hadith 544
16. Al-Jawziyyah. *Ibn Qayyim* (circa. 1340). Arabic. French translation by Bousserouel, Hebri. *Le Paradis: Hadi El Arwah ila biladi El Af'rah.* Paris: Ed. Universel. (2004).
17. Bukhari, Book 55, Hadith 544
18. Bukhari, Book 54, Hadith 468
19. Muslim, Book 40, Hadith 6798
20. Tirmidhi, Book 36, Hadith 2539
21. Tirmidhi, Book 36, Hadith 2545
22. Muslim, Book 40, Hadith 6803

23. Al-Jawziyyah. *Ibn Qayyim* (circa. 1340). Arabic. French translation by Bousserouel, Hebri. *Le Paradis: Hadi El Arwah ila biladi El Af'rah*. Paris: Ed. Universel. (2004).
24. Tirmidhi, Book 36, Book 2539

25. Yahya, H. *Jannah: The Garden from the Qur'an and Hadith*. London: Ta-Ha. (2007).; Imam Ghazzali. *Ihya Ulum ad-Din*, vol. 4.
26. Tirmidhi, Book 36, Hadith 2535
27. Al-Jawziyyah. *Ibn Qayyim* (circa. 1340). Arabic. French translation by Bousserouel, Hebri. *Le Paradis: Hadi El Arwah ila biladi El Af'rah*. Paris: Ed. Universel. (2004).
28. Bukhari, Book 76, Hadith 761; Bukhari, Book 58, Hadith 167; Quran verses 20:117-118
29. Bukhari, Book 3, Hadith 86'
30. Paradise - Jannah - Dr. Reda Bedeir
    http://www.youtube.com/watch?v=TG4hr02kwuU
31. Muslim, Book 40, Hadith 6802
32. Tirmidhi, Book 36, Hadith 2562
33. Al-Ghazali (circa. 1094). *The Remembrance of Death and the Afterlife: Book XL of the Revival of the Religious Sciences*. Translation: Winter, T. J. Cambridge: Islamic Texts Society. (1989).
34. Bukhari, Book 62, Hadith 124
35. Ibn e Majah, Book 37, Hadith 4289
36. Muslim, Book 1, Hadith 384
37. Bukhari Book 72, Hadith 702; Muslim, Book 40, Hadith 6793
38. Tirmidhi, Book 36, Hadith 25444; Yahya, H. *Jannah: The Garden from the Qur'an and Hadith*. London: Ta-Ha. (2007).
39. Tirmidhi, Book 31, Hadith 2240; Sunan Ahmed
40. Bukhari, Book 76, Hadith 527; Muslim, Book 3, Hadith 614
41. Bukhari, Book 60, Hadith 254; Tirmidhi, Book 36, Hadith 2558

Chapter 7

1. Ibn Majah, Book 37, Hadith 4332
2. Muslim, Book 001, Hadith 363
3. 1 Corinthians 2:9
4. Muslim Book 1, Hadith 361
5. Muslim Book 1, Hadith 359
6. Muslim Book 1, Hadith 363
7. Bukhari, Book 76, Hadith 575; Muslim Book 1, Hadith 360
8. Muslim, Book 1, Hadith 361
9. Paradise - By Sheikh Ahmed Ali, http://www.youtube.com/watch?v=FwMMTLGvQZo
10. Muslim, Book 1, Hadith 362
11. Tirmidhi, Book 36, Hadith 2553
12. Muslim Book 40, Hadith 6804; Muslim Book 40, Hadith 6805
13. Bukhari, Book 54, Hadith 466
14. Tirmidhi, Book 36, Hadith 2562
15. Tirmidhi, Book 36, Hadith 2527
16. Yahya, H. *Jannah: The Garden from the Qur'an and Hadith*. London: Ta-Ha. (2007); (Imam Ghazzali, Ihya Ulum ad-Din, vol. 4)
17. Muslim, Book 4, Hadith 1581
18. Muslim, Book 40, Hadith 6793
19. Bukhari, Book 54, Hadith 476
20. Muslim, Book 40, Hadith 6792
21. Tirmidhi, Book 36, Hadith 2536
22. Al-Qurtubi. *At-Tadhkirah*. Translated by Bedeir, R. El-Mansoura: Dar Al-Manarah (Chapter 124, Hadith 418).
23. Tirmidhi, Book 36, Hadith 2563
24. Tirmidhi, Book 36, Hadith 2563
25. Tirmidhi, Book 36, Hadith 2562
26. Yahya, H. *Jannah: The Garden from the Qur'an and Hadith*.

London: Ta-Ha. (2007). (Mukhtasar Tadhkirah al- Qurtubi, p. 333/591)
27. Yahya, H. *Jannah: The Garden from the Qur'an and Hadith*.

London: Ta-Ha. (2007). (Imam Ghazzali, Ihya Ulum ad-Din, vol. 4)
28. Al-Jawziyyah. *Ibn Qayyim* (circa. 1340). Arabic. French translation by Bousserouel, Hebri. *Le Paradis: Hadi El Arwah ila biladi El Af'rah*. Paris: Ed. Universel. (2004).
29. Yahya, H. *Jannah: The Garden from the Qur'an and Hadith*. London: Ta-Ha. (2007). (Mukhtasar Tadhkirah al-Qurtubi, p. 315/522)
30. Yahya, H. Jannah: *The Garden from the Qur'an and Hadith*. London: Ta-Ha. (2007). (Mukhtasar Tadhkirah al-Qurtubi, p. 312/517)
31. Al-Jawziyyah. *Ibn Qayyim* (circa. 1340). Arabic. French translation by Bousserouel, Hebri. *Le Paradis: Hadi El Arwah ila biladi El Af'rah*. Paris: Ed. Universel. (2004); Al-Ghazali (circa. 1094*). The Remembrance of Death and the Afterlife: Book 40 of the Revival of the Religious Sciences*. Translation: Winter, T. J. Cambridge: Islamic Texts Society. (1989).
32. Yahya, H. Jannah: *The Garden from the Qur'an and Hadith*. London: Ta-Ha. (2007). (Mukhtasar Tadhkirah, al-Qurtubi, p. 58)
33. Muslim, Book 2, Hadith 479
34. Tirmidhi, Book 36, Hadith 2542
35. Bukhari Book 93, Hadith 519
36. Al-Jawziyyah. *Ibn Qayyim* (circa. 1340). Arabic. French translation by Bousserouel, Hebri. *Le Paradis: Hadi El Arwah ila biladi El Af'rah*. Paris: Ed. Universel. (2004).
37. Tirmidhi, Book 36, Hadith 2526
38. Tirmidhi, Book 36, Hadith 2525

39. Yahya, H. *Jannah: The Garden from the Qur'an and Hadith*. London: Ta-Ha. (2007), (Mukhtasar Tadhkirah, al-Qurtubi)
40. Bukhari, Book 54, Hadith 474

41. Tafsir Ibn e Kathir, Surah 19:62
42. Paradise - By Sheikh Ahmed Ali, http://www.youtube.com/watch?v=FwMMTLGvQZo
43. Al-Jawziyyah, Ibn Qayyim (circa. 1340). Arabic. French translation by Bousserouel, Hebri. *Le Paradis: Hadi El Arwah ila biladi El Af'rah*. Paris: Ed. Universel. (2004).
44. Tirmidhi, Book 36, Hadith 2564
45. Ibn e Kathir. *The termination of the afflictions and fierce battles*. Translation by Abd El Qadir.
46. Al-Jawziyyah. *Ibn Qayyim* (circa. 1340). Arabic. French translation by Bousserouel, Hebri. *Le Paradis: Hadi El Arwah ila biladi El Af'rah*. Paris: Ed. Universel. (2004).
47. Ibn Majah, Book 1, Hadith 187
48. Al-Jawziyyah. *Ibn Qayyim* (circa. 1340). Arabic. French translation by Bousserouel, Hebri. *Le Paradis: Hadi El Arwah ila biladi El Af'rah*. Paris: Ed. Universel. (2004).

Chapter 8

1. Bukhari, Book 76, Hadith 515
2. *Sahih Muslim*. Translated by Al-Khattab, Nasiruddin. Riyad: Darussalam. (2007). (Book 1, Hadith 265)
3. Description of Paradise (Jennah) - Dr. Ibrahim Dremali. http://www.youtube.com/watch?v=Lt2gSQCa4Tc
4. Muslim Book 1, Hadith 343
5. Ibn e Majah, Book 37, Hadith 4336
6. Ibn e Majah, Book 37, Hadith 4336
7. Ibn e Majah, Book 1, Hadith 184
8. Al-Jawziyyah. *Ibn Qayyim* (circa. 1340). Arabic. French

translation by Bousserouel, Hebri. *Le Paradis: Hadi El Arwah ila biladi El Af'rah*. Paris: Ed. Universel. (2004).
9. Ibid.
10. Ibn e Majah, Book 37, Hadith 4336
11. Description of Paradise (Jennah) - Dr. Ibrahim Dremali. http://www.youtube.com/watch?v=Lt2gSQCa4Tc
12. Bukhari Book 76, Hadith 557

Chapter 9
1. Muslim, Book 40, Hadith 6792; *Sahih Muslim*. Translated by Al-Khattab, Nasiruddin,.Riyad: Darussalam. (2007). (Book 51, Hadith 7146)
2. Muslim, Book 4, Hadith 1416
3. Ibn e Majah, Book 37, Hadith 4336
4. Ibn e Majah, Book 37, Hadith 4336
5. Tirmidhi, Book 36, Hadith 2550
6. Al-Qurtubi. *At-Tadhkirah*. Translated by Bedeir, R. El-Mansoura: Dar Al-Manarah (Chapter 103, Hadith 379).
7. Muslim, Book 40, Hadith 6802
8. Ibn e Majah, Book 37, Hadith 4336
9. Tirmidhi, Book 41, Hadith 2791
10. Tirmidhi, Book 36, Hadith 2544

Chapter. 10
1. Bukhari, Book 39, Hadith 538; Bukhari Book 93, Hadith 610
2. Tirmidhi, Book 36, Hadith 2563
3. Yahya, H. Jannah: *The Garden from the Qur'an and Hadith*. London: Ta-Ha. (2007). (Ahmad Diya ad-Din al-Kamushkhanawi, Ramuz al-Ahadith, vol. 2, p. 366/4)

Chapter 11
1. Muslim, Book 40, Hadith 6778

2. Muslim, Book 39, Hadith 6769
3. Bukhari Book 92, Hadith 384
4. Bukhari, Book 92, Hadith 385; Ahmed, Hadith 7281
5. Bukhari, Book 2, Hadith 42
6. Bukhari, Book 93, Hadith 579; Muslim, Book 5, Hadith 2175
7. Bukhari, Book 55, Hadith 644; Muslim Book 1, Hadith 43
8. Bukhari, Book 2, Hadith 42
9. Tirmidhi, Book 45, Hadith 3540
10. Muslim Book, 35 Hadith 6471
11. Bukhari, Book 54, Hadith 431; Muslim, Book 32, Hadith 6373; Tirmidhi, Book 44, Hadith 3161
12. Bukhari, Book 35, Hadith 6471
13. Bukhari, Book 76, Hadith 509
14. Dawood, Book 2, Hadith 430
15. Bukhari Book 93, Hadith 519
16. Bukhari, Book 4, Hadith 174
17. Bukhari, Book 51, Hadith 28
18. Muslim, Book 1, Hadith 235
19. Muslim, Book 20, Hadith 4688
20. Bukhari, Book 93, Hadith 592
21. Bukhari, Book 43, Hadith 629
22. Muslim, Book 39, Hadith 6757
23. Muslim, Book 30, Hadith 5835
24. Al-Nasai, Book 21, Hadith 2080
25. Spellberg, Denise A. *Thomas Jefferson's Qur'an: Islam and the Founders*. New York: Knopf. (2013).
26. Bukhari, Book 76, Hadith 450; Bukhari Book 93, Hadith 579
27. Tirmidhi, Book 11, Hadith 2441
28. Tirmidhi, Book 11, Hadith 2440
29. Muslim, Book 4, Hadith 2129

Bibliography

Abdul-Hameed, Ali Hasan Ali. *Paradise: Its Blessings and How to Get There* (1999). Translated by Huda Khattab. Riyadh: International Islamic Publishing House. (2006).

Abu Dawud, Imam Hafiz. *Sunan Abu Dawud* (circa. 875). Translated by Yaser Qadhi, Riyadh: Dar-us-Salam. (2008).

Adly, Muhammed Syed. *Al-Jannah* [Paradise]. Hounslow: Message of Islam. (2001).

Ahmad bin Hanbal, Imam. *Musnad Ahmad* (circa. 850). Translated by Nasiruddin Al-Khattab. Riyadh: Dar-us-Salam. (2012).

Alcorn, Randy. *Heaven*. Carol Stream, IL: Tyndale House Publishers. (2004).

Alexander, Eben. *Proof of Heaven: A Neurosurgeon's Journey into the Afterlife*. New York: Simon & Schuster. (2012).

Alighieri, Dante. *The Divine Comedy: Inferno, Purgatorio, Paradiso*. Translated by Allen Mandelbaum. Radford, VA: Wilder Publications. (2011).

Anon. (circa. 1000). *The Subtleties of the Ascension: Lata'if al-Miraj: Early Mystical Sayings on Muhammed's Heavenly Journey*. Translated by Frederick S. Colby. Louisville, KY: Fons Vitae. (2006).

Ashour, Mustafa. *The Jinn in the Qur'an and the Sunna*. London: Dar Al Taqwa Ltd. (1989).

al-Ashqar, Umar. *Al-Jannah Wal Naar* [Paradise and Hell] (1991). Translated by Nasiruddin Al-Khattab. Riyadh: International Islamic Publishing House. (2005).

Aslam, Khawaja Muhammed. The *Spectacle of Death and Glimpses of Life Hereafter*. New Delhi: Adam Publishers. (1992).

Atwater, P.M.H. *Near-Death Experiences, The Rest of the Story: What They Teach Us About Living and Dying and Our True Purpose*. Charlottesville, VA: Hampton Roads Publishing. (2011).

Bah, Alpha Mahmoud (2001). *Glimpses of Life After Death*. Kuala Lumpur: A. S. Noordin. (2010).

Barker, Kenneth. Zondervan NIV Study Bible. Grand Rapids, NI: Zondervan. (2002).

Bediuzzaman Said Nursi. *The Resurrection and the Hereafter: A Decisive Proof of Their Reality*. Clifton, NJ: Tughra Books. (2010).

Belzebuub, V.M.. *Experiencing Astral Travel: An 8-Week Course*. London: Absolute Publishing Group. (2003).

_____. *A Course in Astral Travel and Dreams*. London: Absolute Publishing Group. (2004).

Bruce, Robert and Mercer, Brian. *Mastering Astral Projection: 90-Day Guide to Out-of-Body Experience*. Woodbury, MN: Llewellyn Publications. (2004).

Buhlman, William. *Adventures Beyond the Body: How to Experience Out-of-Body Travel*. New York: Harperone. (1996).

al-Bukhari, Muhammed Ibn Ismail. *Sahih Al-Bukhari* (circa. 850). Translated by Muhammed Muhsin Khan. Riyadh: Dar-us-Salam. (1997).

Burpo, Todd, and Vincent, Lynn. *Heaven Is for Real: A Little Boy's Astounding Story of His Trip to Heaven and Back*. Nashville, TN: Thomas Nelson. (2010).

Carpenter, Harry W. *The Genie Within: Your Subconcious Mind— How It Works and How to Use It*. Harry Carpenter Publishing. (2004).

Carter, Chris. *Science and the Near-Death Experience: How Consciousness Survives Death*. Rochester, VT: Inner Traditions. (2010).

Collins, Francis S. *The Language of God: A Scientist Presents Evidence for Belief*. New York: Simon and Schuster. (2007).

Feynman, Richard P. *QED: The Strange Theory of Light and Matter*. Princeton, NJ: Princeton Science Library. (1988).

Flew, Antony. *There Is A God: How the World's Most Notorious Atheist Changed His Mind*. New York: Harperone. (2008).

Gardner, James. *Intelligent Universe: AI, ET, and the Emerging Mind of the Cosmos*. Pompton Plains, NJ: Career Press/New Page Books. (2007).

al-Ghazali (circa. 1094). *The Remembrance of Death and the Afterlife: Book 40 of the Revival of the Religious Sciences*. Translation: Winter, T. J. Cambridge: Islamic Texts Society. (1989).

Greene, Brian. *The Elegant Universe: Superstrings, Hidden Dimensions, and the Quest for the Ultimate Theory*. New York: W. W. Norton & Company. (2003).

_____. *The Fabric of the Cosmos: Space, Time, and the Texture of Reality*. New York: Vintage Books. (2005).

Haisch, Bernard. The God Theory: *Universes, Zero-Point Fields, and What's Behind It All*. Newburyport, MA: Red Wheel/Weiser. (2006).

Haleem, Abdel. *The Qur'an*. Translation. Oxford: Oxford University Press. (2004).

Hawking, Stephen. *The Universe in a Nutshell*. New York: Bantam. (2001).

_____. *A Briefer History of Time*. New York: Bantam. (2005).
Ibn Kathir, Hafiz.

Al Nehaya fi Fitan wal Malahim [The Termination of the Afflictions and Fierce Battles] (circa. 1350). Translated by Abd El Qader Al Azeez..

Ibn Kathir, Hafiz. *Tafsir Ibn Kathir* (circa. 1350). Translated by Sheikh Safiur-Rahman Al-Mubarakpuri et. al. Riyadh: Dar-us-Salam. (2000).

Ibn Majah, Imam Muhammed Bin Yazeed. *Sunan Ibn Majah* (circa. 875). Translated by Nasiruddin Al-Khattab. Riyadh: Dar-us-Salam. (2007).

Imbrogno, Philip J. *Interdimensional Universe: The New Science of UFOs, Paranormal Phenomena and Otherdimensional Beings.* Woodbury, MN: Llewellyn Publications. (2008).

al-Jawziyyah, Ibn Qayyim (circa. 1340). Arabic. French translation by Bousserouel, Hebri. *Le Paradis: Hadi El Arwah ila biladi El Af'rah.* Paris: Ed. Universel. (2004).

al-Jawziyyah, Ibn Qayyim (circa. 1340). *Kitabar-Ruh: The Soul's Journey After Death.* London: Dar Al Taqwa. (2011).

al-Jibaly, Muhammed Mustafa. *Life in al-Barzakh from Death until Resurrection.* Arlington, TX: Al-Kitaab and As-Sunnah Publishing. (2006).

al-Jilani, Shaikh Abd Al-Qadir: *A Concise Description of Jannah & Jahannam: The Garden of Paradise and the Fire of Hell.* Translated by Holland, Muthar. London: Ta-Ha Publishers. (2010).

Kaku, Michio. *Hyperspace: A Scientific Odyssey Through Parallel Universes, Time Warps, and the 10th Dimension.* Flushing, MI: Anchor. (1995).

_____. *Parallel Worlds: A Journey Through Creation, Higher Dimensions, and the Future of the Cosmos.* Flushing, MI: Anchor. (2006).

_____. *Physics of the Impossible: A Scientific Exploration into the World of Phasers, Force Fields, Teleportation, and Time Travel.* New York: Doubleday. (2008).

al-Kanadi, Abu Bilal Mustafa. *Mysteries of The Soul Expounded.* Birmingham: Al Hidaayah Publishing. (2003).

Kurzweil, Ray. *The Age of Spiritual Machines: When Computers Exceed Human Intelligence.* London: Penguin Books. (2000).

_____. *The Singularity Is Near: When Humans Transcend Biology.* New York: The Viking Press. (2005).

_____. *How to Create a Mind: The Secret of Human Thought Revealed.* New York: The Viking Press. (2012).

Long, Jeffrey. *Evidence of the Afterlife: The Science of Near-Death Experiences.* New York: Harperone. (2010)

Mahmood, Bashirur-Ud-Din. *Mechanics of the Doomsday and Life after Death.* New Delhi: Kitab Bhavan. (2000).

Malik ibn Anas, Imam. *Muwatta Imam Malik* (circa. 775). Translated by Aisha Bewley. Inverness: Madinah Press. (2005).

McTaggart, Lynne. *The Field: The Quest for the Secret Force of the Universe.* New York: Harper. (2003).

Miller, Lisa. *Heaven: Our Enduring Fascination with the Afterlife.* New York: Harper Collins. (2010).

Bibliography   339

Minsky, Marvin. *The Emotion Machine: Commonsense Thinking, Artificial Intelligence, and the Future of the Human Mind*. New York: Simon & Schuster. (2006).

Monroe, Robert. *Ultimate Journey*. Pittsburg, PA: Harmony. (1996).

Moody, Raymond. (1975), *Life After Life*. New York: Harperone. (2001).

_____. *The Light Beyond*. New York: Bantam. (1989).

Muslim Ibn Al-Hajjaj, Imam. *Sahih Muslim* (circa. 850). Translated by Nasiruddin Al-Khattab. Riyadh: Dar-us-Salam. (2007).

Nana, Maulana Abdullah. *Maidens of Paradise*. New Delhi: Idara Impex. (2011).

an-Nasai, Ahmed bin Ali. *Sunan An-Nasai* (circa. 900). Translated by Nasiruddin Al-Khattab, Riyadh: Dar-us-Salam. (2007).

Neil, Mary. *To Heaven and Back: A Doctor's Extraordinary Account of Her Death, Heaven, Angels, and Life Again: A True Story*. Colorado Springs, CO: WaterBrook Press. (2012).

Penrose, Roger. *The Road to Reality: A Complete Guide to the Laws of the Universe*. New York: Knopf. (2005).

Qasmi, Mufti Mohammad Irshad. *The Women of Paradise*. Karachi: Darul-Ishaat. (2007).

al-Qurtabi, Imam Abu Abdullah. *At-Tadhkirah Fiahwalil-Mawta Wal-Akhirah* [In Remembrance of the Affairs of the Dead and Doomsday] (circa. 1250). Translated by Reda Bedeir. El-Mansoura: Dar Al-Manarah. (2004).

Ring, Kenneth. *Lessons from the Light: What We Can Learn from the Near-Death Experience.* Needham, MA: Moment Point Press. (2006)

Ritchie, George. *Return from Tomorrow.* Ada, MI: Revell. (1996).

Rosenblum, Bruce and Kuttner, Fred. *Quantum Enigma: Physics Encounters Consciousness.* Oxford: Oxford University Press. (2008).

Sakr, Ahmad. *Life, Death and the Life After.* Lombard, IL: Foundation for Islamic Knowledge. (1992).

Schroeder, Gerald. *God According to God: A Scientist Discovers We've Been Wrong About God All Along.* New York: Harperone. (2010).

Segal, Alan. *Life After Death: A History of the Afterlife in Western Religion.* New York: Doubleday Religion. (2004).

al-Shimemeri, Abdullah Abdulrahman. *Descriptions of Paradise.* Jeddah: Dar Abul-Qasim. (2010).

Storm, Howard: *My Descent Into Death: A Second Chance at Life.* Pittsburg, PA: Harmony. (2005).

at-Tirmidhi, Imam Hafiz Abu Eisa. *Jami At-Tirmidhi* (circa. 875). Translated by Abu Khaliyl. Riyadh: Dar-us-Salam. (2007).

Unal, Ali. *The Resurrection and the Afterlife*. Somerset, NJ: The Light Inc. (2006).

Van Lommel, Pim. *Consciousness Beyond Life: The Science of the Near-Death Experience*. New York: Harperone. (2010).

Varghese, Roy Abraham. *There Is Life After Death*. Pompton Plains, NJ: Career Press/New Page Books. (2009).

Wiese, Bill. *23 Minutes in Hell: One Man's Story About What He Saw, Heard, and Felt in that Place of Torment*. Lake Mary, FL: Charisma House. (2006).

Yahya, Harun. *Jannah: The Garden from the Qur'an and Hadith*. London: Ta-Ha. (2007). Available from harunyahya.com

Yazbeck Haddad, Yvonne and Idelman Smith, Jane. *The Islamic Understanding of Death and Resurrection*. Oxford: Oxford University Press. (2002).

www.ingramcontent.com/pod-product-compliance
Lightning Source LLC
Chambersburg PA
CBHW030431300426
44112CB00009B/954